Never Land

University of Nebraska Press | Lincoln and London

W. SCOTT OLSEN

Never Land

Adventures, Wonder,
and One World Record
in a Very Small Plane

© 2010 by the Board of Regents of
the University of Nebraska. All rights
reserved. Manufactured in the United
States of America. ∞

Library of Congress Cataloging-
in-Publication Data

Olsen, W. Scott, 1958–
Never land : adventures, wonder, and
one world record in a very small plane
/ W. Scott Olsen.
    p. cm.
Includes bibliographical references.
ISBN 978-0-8032-1750-8 (cloth : alk.
paper)
1. Olsen, W. Scott, 1958– . 2. Air
pilots—United States—Biography.
3. Olsen, W. Scott, 1958– —Travel.
4. Aviation psychology.
I. Title.
TL540.O55A3 2010
629.13092—dc22
[B]
2009031877

Set in Sabon.

For my family

Contents

Acknowledgments   ix

Glossary   xi

Prologue   1

What Remains   6

The Pilot's Journal   31

Altitude   48

A Prairie Roll   60

Bad Form   79

Dreams of Flying   89

The Spin   107

The World Record   115

The Long Cross-Country   151

A Note on Sources   185

Acknowledgments

Flying is a leap into the extraordinary. Without the help of extraordinary people, this book would not exist. Pat Valdata, Jake Gust, Joanna Spiekermeier, and Mark Malmberg—each of them fine pilots—read early versions of some chapters and provided invaluable advice and suggestions. Daryl Ritchison gave me weather advice well in front of any forecast and was always right. The David Clark company kept me sane by providing a noise-canceling x-11 headset, and the Big Head Hat company kept me warm and shaded by providing caps. Concordia College and the Department of English at Concordia College provided financial support for the expensive business of flying, as did Concordia alum Robert Heuer. Annette Wenda has the best ear of any copyeditor on the planet, and I am lucky to be under her care. Robert Taylor, my editor at Nebraska, is an unfailing source of encouragement—especially when the weather keeps me on the ground and thus the manuscript off schedule. To each of these people I offer a profound thank-you.

Special mention needs to be given to Mike Paulson, manager of the Fargo Flight School, and the Fargo Jet Center. Mike fielded a thousand questions with patience and insight, and the Jet Center is simply the best FBO in the country.

Parts of this book have appeared in literary magazines: "A Prairie Roll" appeared as "Aileron Jazz" in *Mid-American Review*; "What Remains" appeared in *Nimrod: International Journal of Prose and Poetry*; "Altitude" was published in the *North American Review*; and "The World Record" appeared in *Mid-American Review*. A small section of "The World Record" also appeared in the magazine *Outside Go*. "The Long Cross-Country" appeared in the *Northwest Review*. I am grateful to the editors of all these fine journals for their support and interest.

Finally, the deepest thanks goes to my wife, Maureen, and to our kids, Kate and Andrew, for their love and patience when the sky called.

Glossary

AGL: Altitude above ground level.

Airspeed: The speed of the air moving over an airplane's wing (usually given in knots).

ATC: Air Traffic Control.

ATIS: Automatic Terminal Information Service, an automated reporting service used by pilots to obtain current information on weather conditions, active runways, available approaches, and so forth.

AWOS: Another automated weather reporting service.

Flight Service: Run by Lockheed Martin, a service that pilots use to say where they are flying (file a flight plan) and to obtain important information about weather and other conditions along that route. One of the elements of a flight plan is the "time en route." If a pilot exceeds it by more than a half hour, Flight Service will call the destination airport to see if the pilot simply forgot to close the flight plan. But if the pilot has not landed, the search teams organize.

Ground speed: The speed that the airplane is moving over the ground (usually given in knots).

IFR: Instrument flight rules.

Information xxx: Weather changes rapidly. Automated systems update themselves quickly. An automated weather system such as the ATIS, which is broadcast using a human voice generator over radio waves, will conclude its report with something like, "Upon contacting tower, report you have information Alpha" or "information Bravo." That way the tower knows you have the most current information regarding wind speed and direction, visibility, and so forth.

METAR: Code used by weather reporting stations to report current weather conditions at airports. A METAR reading looks like this: KFAR 031653Z 18013KT 10SM CLR 01M03 A2954 RMK AO2 SLP014 T00061028. "KFAR" is the reporting station (in this case Fargo, North Dakota). "031653Z" represents the day of the month (in this case the third), and the time is 1653 Zulu. ("Zulu" is the military designation for Greenwich [England] mean time and is equivalent to 10:35 a.m. in the central time zone of the United States.) "18013KT" means that the wind is from 180 degrees on the compass (from the south) at 13 knots. A letter G here would indicate gust speeds. "10SM" means that the visibility is at least 10 statute miles (this is normally the maximum number given). "CLR" means clear skies. This space can read BLSN for blowing snow, TR for thunderstorm, and so on. "01M03" means that the temperature is 1°C and the dew point is minus 3°C. (It is important to know the dew point, because if the temperature and the dew point are 4 or fewer degrees apart and there is little or no wind, there is probably fog.) "A2954" is the air pressure, which is used to set the altimeter reading. This is a constantly changing value, so ATC and the towers give frequent altimeter updates. "AO2" is the type of weather reporting equipment in use.

MSL: Altitude above mean sea level.

TAF: Terminal Area Forecast.

VRF: Visual flight rules.

VOR: A type of radio beacon that pilots use to navigate toward or away from and establish their positions. ATC can "see" a VOR and all the air traffic near it on its radar screens.

A Note on Numbers

In general, numbers are spelled out as complete words in this book because of the way pilots talk to each other and to control towers. In stating a radio frequency of 122.8 mhz, for example, a pilot would never say "one hundred and twenty-two point eight." That's too easily confusing over the air. So it's always "one two two point eight." The tail number of the plane I fly most in this book could be typed as "N5329B." But it's always spoken as "November Five Three Two Nine Bravo." The shorthand for this is "Two Nine Bravo," not "29B" (or "twenty-nine B").

Runway numbers are their compass heading, but you need to add a zero to the end of the number. A runway number of "three-six," for example, would be pointing toward 360 degrees on the compass, or due north.

Prologue

Here is what I believe.

We have a *desire* for infinity.

Nature, the axiom goes, abhors a vacuum. Nature will fill any vacuum, by any means, as quickly as possible. Nature rushes to fill the empty space, compelled to find a way, any way at all, to leap toward distance. This is why I believe there is nothing in the long line of human inventions as deeply rooted in our souls as the airship. It doesn't matter if the airship is a balloon, a kite, a glider, a zeppelin, a little Cessna 152, or the x-15. No building, no monument, no bridge, no wheel or aqueduct, no lightbulb or computer system comes even close to the spirit, the hope, the necessity, and the reach of flying. Up has always been a better direction than down. Heaven is always someplace above where we are now. To look up into a clear or cloud-filled sky and to ask "How do I get *there?*" is one of our ancient questions.

Curiosity, and the reaching that comes with it, has a million expressions. Climbing a mountain is the expression of wondering what limits there are to rock. The sailing ship is the way we discover how far the ocean goes. The submarine is the way we discover how deep. And it is certainly possible that these are all really the same thing, all ways of our reaching out to fill the void. Perhaps the submarine is in fact the mirror reflection of the airship, everything the same except it's all backward. Down instead of up. Fully enclosed against increasing pressure instead of open to thinning air. And perhaps the sailing ship is very much like the airship, curving the wind to catch it in its upright wings and move it forward. All three machines, and the people who steer them, navigating a fluid alive with currents and storms as well as soul-exploding beauty.

But, in truth, I think not. The sailing ship ends on the other side of the ocean. The submarine ends at the ocean floor. Even the climber must turn around when the summit has been gained. At the moment of departure, there is a finite goal, a limit, a boundary that is imposed by geography and inviolate.

Only the airship can claim a step toward infinity. Only the airship pilot can look up and find a universe larger than his ability to dream it.

When I imagine flying, as I often do, I imagine four moments. The first is when the preflight checks are done, the routes planned and the flight plan filed, the last sip of coffee drained, and the engine finally running. This is the moment of declaration. This is when you announce to the world that you are in an airplane and you are ready to fly. You look around the cockpit, just making sure, and then you key the microphone. "Fargo Ground," you say, if you are flying the little Cessna 152 where I took my lessons, "this is Cessna Five Three Two Nine Bravo. I'm at the north ramp, departing to the west, at or below four thousand feet, information Juliet." The controller in the tower at Fargo's Hector Field will reply, give you a runway to head for and a squawk code for the transponder, which you will say back to confirm, and then your toes will come off the brakes and the airplane will start to roll. The music is playing, so to speak, and the dance has begun. You have stated your intentions and stepped out onto the floor.

The second moment is not even a few minutes later. Just before the runway there is a place to hold for other traffic, to run up your engine and make sure all systems are working, and when you are done you call the tower again, but on a different frequency for a different purpose. "Fargo Tower," you say, "this is Cessna Five Three Two Nine Bravo, ready for takeoff." "Cessna Five Three Two Nine Bravo," the controller will respond, "you are cleared for takeoff, runway one-eight." There might be other instructions, such as to maintain runway heading after takeoff, or to make an immediate turn one way or the other, but you push the throttle in and taxi onto the runway. You point the nose down the centerline, and then push the throttle in all the way hard. The engine deepens its voice. The airplane shudders a little as it beings to roll, faster and then faster still, and you watch the runway centerline to make sure you're heading straight. You also watch one instrument, the airspeed indicator, because when it gets to a certain number, for me about 60 knots, the second moment happens. When the plane is going fast enough, you pull back on the wheel or stick and the nose of the airplane rises. It's called rotation. You point the thing at the sky. And into the sky it goes.

The third moment is in the landing. If it's a normal day and the winds aren't too wicked, you've entered the airport traffic pattern on the downwind leg and watched the runway parallel the airplane. When the runway numbers are about 45 degrees behind your shoulder, you turn onto the short base leg, and then onto final approach. You bleed off the last bits of altitude and airspeed, and as the runway numbers come under your tires you should be low enough and slow enough to level off and then flare, to point the nose back to the sky even though the plane is descending, and then there is that feeling of the tires meeting pavement. You are no longer flying. No matter what else, you have landed an airplane. That moment, the tires meeting runway, is the finale, the signal of a job well done, the point where your smile is relaxed. You want to hurry to the hangar or the tie-down spot, because everything that's just happened, even if all you did was fly the pattern for touch-and-goes, is now a story to tell. And you know there are people in the hangar who will listen.

But the fourth moment is the important one. It is unlike the others in nearly every way. It is special, and it's going to take me this entire book to explain. The fourth moment rises gradually, quietly, and while it has very little to do with technique or physics or meteorology, it has everything to do with intimacy and how well a pilot knows the plane he or she is flying. The fourth moment is when the airplane as an object ceases to exit. The fourth moment is when the airplane becomes, instead, an extension of the self. When you can feel the rush of air over the wings and past the rudder.

When you can feel, in your hands and in your legs, the body moving in the sky. The fourth moment, which does not always happen, is the first moment you can say you are truly flying. Just as there is a subtle though obvious difference between following instruction and real dancing, between technique and art, there is a moment in the air when you understand that, this day at least, you belong where you are. And a small voice in the back of your head, childlike yet fully aware, lets you know that if this day were truly perfect, you would never land.

What Remains

There has to be something—

Painted barn tops. The rusty skeleton of a tower that once held a beacon. Marks on the land, now plowed and harvested for nearly eighty years. But if they are here, I cannot find them.

The altimeter in this little Cessna 152, tail number Five Three Two Nine Bravo, says I am two thousand five hundred feet above sea level, and over this part of the North Dakota prairie that means one thousand six hundred feet above the ground. Yet it's a beautiful spring day, and I can see to every horizon. The wind is from the north at only 3 knots. The sun is shining. There was some ground fog earlier, but now there is just a haze in the air—some showers on the radar, off to the west and north, but they are light. The rain may not even reach the ground.

It has been almost a year since I sat in a pilot's seat, and the feel of this small airplane in my hands and feet is a reintroduced joy and grace. Last night, going over the calculations for weight and balance, the need for fuel, planning my route, looking at the weather, I smiled at how easily the mind can switch from one set of borders to another. Last night, early, I was thinking about small repairs I need to make around the house, about the thousand chores that need to be done. My world was limited, scarcely larger than the three-mile walk I take with our collie. But when I retrieved my flight bag from a bookshelf and unfolded a sectional map, the world became a much larger place. Instantly, the definition of *here* included magnetic deviations and airspace rules, winds aloft at three thousand and six thousand feet, reported from a thousand different locations. *Here* was everything within about three hundred miles of where I sat. All of it present. All of it necessary. *Here*, whatever that space is in the brain, suddenly included the curve of the earth.

And today, what I am wondering is if *here*, which is nearly the same word as *now*, can include decades of time, time long passed. I have been wondering about the first pilots in this region, the old airmail pilots, and how they saw the land. How they found their way from one place to another. I have a global positioning system (GPS) and radio navigation. I would have to work to get lost. They had neither, and getting lost not only was possible but could very well be lethal. Follow the land, the rivers and the roads. Beware of haze, of mist, of clouds—anything that could send you off course.

In the old days, I have learned, there were barn tops painted with arrows pointing to airports. There were flashing beacons every fifteen miles for navigation at night. There were intermediate landing fields, too, just pastureland made available for emergencies. And all through this past winter, every cold and windy night slamming itself against the windows and siding of my house, I have been wondering if any of those first things have survived. Is there a barn, old and gray and leaning tremendously to one side or another, with a faded arrow on its roof? Is there a plowed shape in the ground that would tell me this place was once a landing field? You would see these things only from the air. Every time I laced up my winter boots, I knew a little more deeply that I would have to find out.

What I am looking for, of course, is evidence, some small piece of the *then* that has made it through to the *now*. And I am looking for that moment of encounter.

What I am looking for is the connection between history and self—hard and physical and real in a way that notes from an index in some corner of a library will never be—the very same thing that people look for when they retrace the route of Lewis and Clark or Marco Polo, when they stand on the stone of the Colosseum or in the grass at Gettysburg, when they find themselves in Jerusalem or Delhi or Machu Picchu or Auschwitz or the Olduvai Gorge. How would I have measured up? Who would I have been? The time between then and now is very large, and my life is very short. I need to know.

. . .

Start with 1918—

World War I is four years old. The Russian Constituent Assembly is dissolved by the Bolsheviks, Czar Nicholas II and his family are executed, and the Germans bomb Paris. The Allies begin a new offensive on the western front. The U.S. Post Office burns magazine selections of James Joyce's

Ulysses, H. L. Mencken publishes *In Defense of Women*, and there are new books by Aldous Huxley, D. H. Lawrence, Bertrand Russell, and H. G. Wells. Paul Klee is at work, as are Freud and Jung. Claude Debussy dies, and Leonard Bernstein is born. The Dada movement begins. There is new music by Béla Bartók, Irving Berlin, Jerome Kern, and Igor Stravinsky, and Max Planck wins the Nobel Prize for Physics for introducing quantum theory. Vilhjalmur Stefansson returns from five years of exploring north of the Arctic Circle. A horse named Exterminator wins the Kentucky Derby, and Knute Rockne is named head football coach at Notre Dame. Missouri is the last state to ratify the compulsory school attendance law. Daylight savings time begins. Billy Graham is born. Jack Dempsey knocks out Carl Morris in fourteen seconds. Eight and a half million people have died in the war; twenty-one million have been wounded. An outbreak of influenza begins that turns into a worldwide pandemic that kills nearly twenty-two million.

It is a difficult year, and a tremendous year as well. Disaster and the work of creation. Chaos, and then a renewed sense of purpose. Perhaps a desire to make things better after they have gone so terribly wrong.

On April 21, 1918, Manfred von Richthofen, the Red Baron, the most successful ace of World War I, is shot down and killed. Chasing one Sopwith Camel and being chased by another, he takes a bullet through his heart and lungs, and still manages to land his Fokker without damage. Although there is some question, it's most likely the bullet comes from the ground. He is buried with full military honors by his enemies, the British and Australians, and a British pilot flies over German territory to drop the news.

Not even one month later, on the other side of the planet, another era starts. Less dramatically, awkwardly but insistently, airmail begins in the United States. This too will change the planet.

Airmail. Like our visions of the Pony Express, the very *idea* of airmail fills our heads with images of daring pilots on noble missions. Fast news from the outside, delivered selflessly and at great risk, regularly and on time. The fighter pilots of World War I were heroes, battling an enemy, finding victory because of better skill, better equipment, better luck. But the airmail pilots were extraordinary. You couldn't outwit a thunderstorm. You couldn't surprise a blizzard or shoot down the fog. You made it through, or didn't, only by what seemed like the grace of God. Charles Lindbergh was an airmail pilot, and even he had to bail out twice and float to earth under a parachute because of weather.

In the introduction to a book called *Pilot's Directions*, William Leary writes, "The country's first regularly scheduled airmail service opened with great fanfare on May 15, 1918. Even President Woodrow Wilson took time off from his demanding wartime responsibilities to attend the inaugural. At 11:46 a.m., Lt. George L. Boyle departed Washington's Polo Field with 140 pounds of mail for Philadelphia and New York. Unfortunately, the young pilot became lost en route when he followed the wrong railroad tracks out of Washington. Attempting to land to get directions, Boyle managed to nose over, flipping the Jenny on its back. To [Assistant Postmaster] Praeger's great chagrin, the mail went by train."

Not the best beginning. And Boyle didn't just follow the wrong tracks. Three days later, he was given a bit of advice he followed exactly. Keep Chesapeake Bay on your right, he was told. But then the north end of Chesapeake Bay showed up, and he followed the other side, always keeping the water of the bay on his right, until he landed in Cape Charles, out of gas and out of land, in completely the wrong place. But it was a start nonetheless. Other flights followed, and a little later that same year, the first New York to Chicago route was opened. Flying time: ten hours and five minutes.

. . .

If I were driving this route, the names of towns would come to me in order: Fargo, Harwood, Argusville, Gardner, Grandin. Places and people I know, events that can be marked in the soil. Flying, however, means a different perspective. Even just a couple thousand feet up the world needs to be rethought. Altitude brings the surface together. Pilots still mark waypoints, towns and structures and physical earth identifiable from the air, and they mark the time it takes to fly between them to make sure the plane is on course. Before takeoff, with a check of the winds and some fast calculations on a computer or a type of circular slide rule called an E6B, a pilot knows, for example, it should take eighteen minutes to fly from Town A to Town B. If Town B shows up too early or too late, or on the wrong side of the airplane, or does not show up at all, the pilot can keep track of where the plane's shadow falls and correct what needs to be fixed.

But to be honest, from the air the towns do not seem so separate, their buildings and their stories more mingled than apart. The Red River, old and meandering, cuts back and loops and winds. Smaller rivers, usually invisible to the roadways, join the Red from both sides. In 1997, there was a flood here that made world news. The land is flat, the bottom of the Pleistocene-era Lake Agassiz, the largest inland sea in the earth's history, and this river is the remainder of its drainage. When seven blizzards dropped more than one hundred inches of snow that winter, the spring melt became a problem. The Red flows north, and when the southern end thaws the northern end is still ice locked. The water has nowhere to go, so it spreads over the prairie. Following a river is one of the earliest forms of airplane navigation. At altitude, following a river with history is to see the connections and to feel afresh a sense of humility.

I have been away from flying long enough that I want someone with me, to make sure I remember what I think I remember, and so Joanna, an instructor from the Fargo Jet Center, sits in the right seat today. We take off, the plane a light dance in my hands as the wheels leave the ground and we make the short jog over to the river. If you had to follow something to Pembina, to mark your route, the river would be the first best choice. Because I am flying, Joanna gets to do something rare for a flight instructor—she gets to look around. She knows what we're looking for, and she's eager to find something. We call out to each other what we see.

"That's a pretty farmstead," I say.

"Look at that wooden bridge!" she says.

"It's all *new* barns and Quonset huts," I say. "I don't see a single old barn."

This is early May, and the fields are all brown. Snow and ice still hide in the shadowed spots. We see farmers out tilling the land, plowing and planting.

. . .

Now imagine 1921—

Warren Harding is inaugurated as the twenty-ninth president of the United States. Hitler's storm troopers begin a program of terror. Enrico Caruso dies. Sacco and Vanzetti are found guilty of murder. The first radio broadcast of a baseball game is heard from the Polo Grounds in New York. The Ku Klux Klan is openly violent. Charlie Chaplin stars in *The Kid*.

In just three years, airmail has grown from one local route into the opening of a breathtaking transcontinental airway. New York to San Francisco via Cleveland, Chicago, Omaha, Cheyenne, Salt Lake City, Elko, and Reno. Just like the Pony Express with their horses, an airmail pilot would fly one leg, land, and a relief pilot would hurry into the cockpit, ready to fly the next stage, to keep the mail going. And just like the Pony Express, many pilots die working out the routes, fighting their machines, dodging the weather. The *New York Sun* runs an editorial that calls the route "homicidal insanity." Yet the biggest problem is night. Pilots cannot find their way over the mountains at night, so the mail is transferred from airplane to train and then back, and the total time savings turns out to be not very much at all.

But night is only a problem to be solved. And the solution is the prairie. Begin in the morning on either coast, and you cross the mountains in daylight. To fly the nighttime prairie, it seems, all you need is a good sense of direction. And between Cheyenne and Chicago, the post office has built 616 flashing beacons, one every three miles, to light the way. So on February 22, 1921, four airmail planes are sent out to demonstrate the night-flying abilities of the new transcontinental airway, to ensure the speed of delivery the idea has promised. Two leave New York, bound for San Francisco. Only one makes it to Chicago, where the continuation is canceled because of bad weather. Two leave San Francisco, bound for New York. One crashes in Nevada, and the pilot, William Lewis, is killed.

But one plane makes it through. As evening falls, a pilot named Frank Yeager takes over the controls of the De Havilland DH-4 biplane in Salt Lake City and flies via Cheyenne to North Platte, Nebraska. In North Platte, he gives the airplane to a man named James "Jack" Knight, and at 10:44 p.m. Knight leaves the ground, heading for Omaha.

What happens next is the stuff that creates a legend. People on the ground know the flight is coming, and somehow know the route. They certainly know the weather. And suddenly there are bonfires lit along the way to guide the pilot! No signal more ancient, no signal more welcome, no history book says how this was planned. No text explains what it must have been like, standing outside in midwinter, tending a fire, listening for the sound of one small airplane in the sky.

In Omaha, the replacement pilot either fails to appear or refuses to fly. The weather is cold, below zero, and turning nasty with snowfall and fog. For whatever reason, Knight decides to fly on himself. His takeoff time is 1:59 a.m. The plan is to stop in Des Moines, but deep snow prevents a landing. He flies on to the emergency field in Iowa City, where the night watchman lights railroad flares to aid the landing. Across Iowa and then Illinois, through bad weather slowly turning better, he finds Chicago's Checkerboard Field and a crowd of people who have turned out to see him land. A hero's welcome at 8:40 a.m. In the history books, the scholars say this one flight kept airmail alive.

. . .

Published in 1921, *Pilot's Directions: New York–San Francisco Route* is exactly that: directions for pilots flying the first transcontinental airmail route. But instead of radio beam or GPS, these directions are all ground based. The first section, New York to Bellefonte, begins this way:

Miles.

0. *Hazelhurst Field, Long Island.*—Follow the tracks of the Long Island Railroad past Belmont Park race track, keeping Jamaica on the left. Cross New York over the lower end of Central Park.

25. *Newark, N.J.*—Heller Field is located in Newark and may be identified as follows: The field is 1¼ miles west of the Passaic River and lies in the V formed by the Greenwood Lake Division and Orange branch of the New York, Lake Erie & Western Railroad. The Morris Canal bounds the western edge of the field. The roof of the large steel hangar is painted an orange color.

30. *Orange Mountains.*—Cross the Orange Mountains over a small round lake or pond. Slightly to the right will be seen the polo field and golf course of Essex Country Club. About 8 miles to the north is Mountain Lake, easily seen after crossing the Orange Mountains.

No maps. No sectional charts. No radio beacons. No VOR or automatic direction finder. Just a pocket-sized book of directions. Fly from this river to those railroad tracks, turn south, follow the tracks until you see the city, turn west, and there should be a notch in the mountains. Cross the whole country this way. Good luck.

. . .

In a light-brown field, wide dark paths mark where a tractor has been, pulling disks or plows. But the paths loop and curl and cut back on each other, ramble all over the section like a drunk's wandering after too long at the bar. Farmers checking their land, wondering if the fields are dry enough to plant, turning to earth to look just under the surface.

Joanna spots a beautiful green home, with porches and decks and a rounded turret room, too. She finds bridges and then drainage pipes in ditches. She spots bright-green tanks that could hold water or feed for livestock. The river is nothing but bends and twists, riparian trees shading the banks. We talk about the trees that make the ruler-straight shelterbelts for farmers, and about the evergreens that appear in the incongruous cemeteries, about how only the burr oak is native to this part of the prairie. Looking out her side window, she finds a point on the river where the grasses have been burned, black earth with some gray ash mounds still smoking.

But no painted barn tops. No beacons. No signs in the earth. My own eyes are fixed over the nose of the plane, looking for what might appear in the distance, looking for what type of aid or invitation there might be.

The winds have come up, 17 knots of headwind against the plane. Looking at the interstate highway, I watch a semitruck pass us heading north. We have to land in Grand Forks for gas, to have enough to get us to Pembina and back, so we call Grand Forks Approach and let them know we're

WHAT REMAINS

coming in. I ask for a route that lets us stay over the river for as long as possible. The request is approved, but still there is nothing.

. . .

Sometimes it's tough to get a handle on things.

On the Web, from an official North Dakota government site, I read, "1928: An air mail service between the Twin Cities and Winnipeg through North Dakota was inaugurated, and Carl Ben Eielson of Hatton [North Dakota] became the first person to fly nonstop over the arctic."

1928. The year Amelia Earhart becomes the first woman to fly across the Atlantic. New music includes Gershwin's *American in Paris* and Ravel's *Boléro*. The first Mickey Mouse films appear. D. H. Lawrence publishes *Lady Chatterley's Lover*.

But also on the Web there is an envelope for sale. Theodore Wolke of Prospect Avenue in New York sends a letter to Peggy Wolke of the same address. The letter is dated February 2, 1931, and the postmark is Fargo, North Dakota, at 11:00 a.m. The postage stamp costs five cents. Above Peggy's address "Via Air Mail" is typed in all capital letters. Above Theodore's return address, on neatly printed stationery, "Chicago—St. Paul Route. A.M. #9" is also typed. Most strikingly, however, is the large mark below the return address. A circle that fills nearly half the envelope, the outer ring reads "First Flight * Twin Cities–Pembina Extension * Route A.M. 9 * P.O.D. * Air Mail." Inside the ring there's a picture of a small airplane flying over the trees and fields and buildings of what is labeled as the State Agricultural College, under the banner of "Fargo, N.Dak., Feb. 21 1931."

1931. The year Al Capone is jailed for income tax evasion, the north face of the Matterhorn is climbed, and Knute Rockne dies in an airplane crash. Salvador Dalí paints *The Persistence of Memory*, and Boris Karloff stars in *Frankenstein*. The Empire State Building is finished, and the building of Rockefeller Center begins. Pilots Clyde Pangborn and Hugh Herndon fly nonstop from Japan to Washington State in forty-one hours.

Clearly, this was an important day, a cause for celebration and remembrance. But how can there be a first flight in 1928 and another first flight in 1931?

On the phone with the staff and volunteers at the Northwest Airlines History Office, I hear a story too good to be true, and perfectly believable. On February 1, 1928, Northwest became an international airline by starting weekly service to Winnipeg, Manitoba. Three months later, however, the service was stopped because of opposition from the Canadian government. Then on February 2, 1931, the service was resumed. A compromise had been worked out to satisfy both countries. Northwest would fly the cargo and passengers from Minneapolis to Fargo, then Grand Forks, then north to the border town of Pembina, North Dakota, where they would be met by a plane from Western Canada Airways that would take them the remaining few miles.

But February 2, 1931, was Groundhog Day, and the groundhog did not see his shadow. The fog was dense and everywhere on the prairie. Joe Ohrbeck, the pilot for Northwest, made it only as far as Osakis, Minnesota, before he had to land the plane. He didn't even make it to Fargo. The Canadian pilots never left the ground. The eighteen thousand letters in the cargo hold of Ohrbeck's plane had to wait until the next day to reach Canada.

What news did Theodore send to Peggy? In Fargo, that letter waited, stamped in celebration, for an airplane that would not arrive until the weather cleared.

. . .

The stop in Grand Forks is fast and pleasant. Hot coffee in the flight support office, some candy from a little dish at the desk. We add only four gallons of gas, but that's nearly an hour of flying time. Once back in the air, we angle toward the river and keep watching.

"How easy," I ask, "do you think it would have been to get lost?"

At one level, we are flying over Thomas Jefferson's dream. Section roads run straight north–south and straight east–west. There are small turns and burps where the earth refused to give way or some creek made a mess of things, but mainly the world looks like an ordered grid, easy to measure. You can count off the miles to infinity. It would be possible to follow one road for a very long time. But in haze, or punching through just one cloud, you couldn't be sure the road you're following now is the road you began to follow earlier. If you let your attention wander, even just a little, you could be lost over a land that is perfectly ordered, and thus perfectly unknowable.

"You have the river," Joanna says. "I could never be lost here."

"Yes, but what if you got away from it?"

"I would never do that. If I had to fly here in those days,

I would lock this river right out my window and never lose sight of it."

She is right, of course. Navigation, to a pilot, is one of the basics, like having a propeller. And unlike the parts of the machine that takes you into the air, navigation speaks to the pilot's understanding of the three-dimensional world, to the pilot's skill and artistry. If you get lost, you can't pull over and ask directions. If you run out of gas, you can't just pull to the side and make a telephone call.

If I were flying in the early days, I would be focused on the flying. I would make sure my cargo of letters and packages made it safely to wherever it was destined to go. I would hear the echo of the post office motto, "Neither rain, nor snow, nor . . . ," and it would keep me on task with its noble promise. But I can be easily distracted. There is a farm in the distance, a farmer working the fields, white tanks of anhydrous ammonia parked fieldside. I cannot see if he is just turning the earth, or if he is pulling planters as well, and there is a part of me that wants to go look.

"Look at this!" Joanna cries out.

In the field below us, it looks like large letter *V*s have been cut at the fencerow, angling toward the middle. It looks like an arrow, or a pointer, cut into the ground. We both wonder out loud if this could have been an intermediate field, a safe haven for a sudden worry, marked for the aerial view. We make a steep turn to the right, circling over the site. But then we see another field, close by, with the same markings. Then another. In a few days, my friend Jake Gust will tell me that this is what a field looks like from the air when a farmer works his land by driving the perimeter, then the next inside circuit, then the next, instead of back and forth across the length or breadth. From the air, a rectangular field looks like the back of an envelope with the flap sealed down, or like the slopes of the roof of a house.

And even a few days later, I will discover that Joanna and I aren't even looking at the same thing. In an e-mail she will write, "You didn't see what I was looking at because what you referred to was the arrows that the tractors leave in the fields and I saw that too, but more interesting, what I saw was three, long, green strips of grass located directly in the backyard of a house, I described them as miniature runways, or runways for model airplanes. But the shape they formed was very distinctive and the three lines all came into a peak that looked like an arrow pointing north, northwest. Perhaps they were strips for model airplanes or just a design the family wanted in their backyard, but it seemed to me the only thing that could have or may have possibly been from the old mail route. Do you know what I am talking about?"

Today, though, one thousand five hundred feet above the ground, Joanna and I wonder if this could be that thing that remains, even though we are seeing different things. Hope fills the little airplane. Then, sadly, we turn the airplane north again. We are almost to Pembina.

. . .

On my desk is a photocopied section from a 1920 publication called *Municipal Landing Fields and Air Ports*, sent to me by a historian at the National Air and Space Museum Library. The directory lists eighteen airports in North Dakota. Bismarck and Fort Lincoln are listed as Government Fields, under the control of the federal government. The remaining sixteen—Dickinson, Eagles Nest, Eldridge, Fargo,

Glen Ullin, Grand Forks, Hobart, Jamestown, Judson, Mandan, Sedalia, Sims, Sunny, Sweet Briar, Valley City, and Williston—are listed as Emergency Fields, "at which landings have been made but where no facilities exist for obtaining supplies."

Also on my desk, also photocopied and also from the Air and Space Museum, a 1939 directory, *Airports: Established Landing Fields and Seaplane Bases in the United States*, that includes a map of the now thirty-nine airports in North Dakota. Following the airmail route, I see that Fargo has become a Municipal Field, the highest ranking. Valley City is a Department of Commerce Intermediate Field. Jamestown is Municipal. Medina is Auxiliary. Dawson is Intermediate. Steele is Auxiliary. Bismarck is Municipal. Just to the south of the route, there is an Auxiliary Field in Streeter, then a Municipal Field in Deisem. Just to the north, Auxiliary Fields in Erie and Carrington.

In my hands, though, is the current edition of the *U.S. Government Airport Facility Directory*, which lists more than one hundred landing fields in North Dakota. But the landing field at Medina is gone, as are Dawson, Steele, Streeter, Deisem, and Erie.

. . .

What I am looking for, in truth, is stories.

The guys at the Northwest Airlines History Office give me a phone number, a pilot named Joe Kimm, who joined Northwest in 1929 as a flight steward, running cabin service inside a twelve-passenger Ford Tri-Motor airplane when he was seventeen years old. Two days later, we are on the phone with each other.

"I had been building model airplanes since I was ten years old," Joe tells me, "and then a pilot for Northwest Airways named Walter Bullock wrote an article about the Ford Tri-Motor model for *Popular Mechanics* and suddenly found himself making parts and kits in his basement."

Ninety-six years old, his voice and mind as strong as ever, Joe is telling me how his flying career began.

"I won the indoor competition of a citywide model airplane contest in Minneapolis in 1928, in December, about a month before I graduated from high school in January 1929. There were about fifteen or twenty of us in a model airplane club we formed, and one of them knew Walter Bullock. Walter was about twenty-seven years old, had begun flying in 1915, worked for Northwest since 1927. Walter came to the first club meeting and said he needed help. I had just quit a job that paid me twelve dollars a week. Walter said he'd pay me twelve dollars a week to help with the kits. It was through Walter that I learned about flight stewards, and I said if he'd let me do that I'd work on my days off for nothing.

"In June, Northwest lost its first airplane. It crashed on the bluff in St. Paul. The pilot was killed, but the flight steward, Bob Johnson, was only mildly injured. So three days after the accident Walter tells me I can fly with him to Chicago as a flight steward if I got my parents' permission.

"I went to Mother, and I said, 'Mom, I'm all excited. Walter says I can go with him to Chicago tomorrow morning if I get your permission.' And she said, 'Oh, son, you better ask your father.' So I went to Dad, and I said, 'Dad, Walter says I can go with him to Chicago tomorrow if I get your permission.' And he looked at me and said, 'Oh, son, you better ask your mother.' And that was it. I decided they weren't objecting, so I got up in the morning and went out to the airport to take my first flight. Incidentally, I had gone to the hospital the night before to pick up Bobby Johnson's uniform. I needed a uniform to wear, and he was about the same tall, gangly kid I was, and his uniform fit me fine.

"I got to the airport, and they gave me a box of money and tickets, because there was no ticket counter out there— they only sold tickets downtown—and I had to sell tickets if anyone came to the airport and needed one. I never did sell a ticket. The next thing they did was instruct me that I had to wear a pistol. So they gave me a .38 revolver with a holster and belt and told me to put that around my waist and wear it. I had to wear this because I was handling registered mail, and it was a requirement of the post office that everyone handling registered mail had to be armed. I had never fired a gun before, and they didn't even tell me how to load it or fire it! They just handed me the gun. There's been a lot of controversy in recent years about arming pilots, but back then they had no problem giving a gun to a seventeen-year-old kid. I carried that same gun for twelve years and turned it in when I went into the service. But I had decided that if anyone wanted the airmail, all they had to do was tell me where to put it and I'd take it there for them."

I tell Joe I can't imagine going to the hospital to pick up the uniform of a man who had been in an airplane crash so I could fly in his place, or carrying a gun to protect the mail, and he laughs. "That's just the way it was back then," he says.

"Along about the beginning of 1930," he continues, "I decided I had the wrong job. I was busier than hell, doing all the work for $78 a month, and the pilot, all he did was sit up front and he got $700. So I decided I had to learn to fly. In 1930 there wasn't any money. The crash in October of '29 had really put the country in the kibosh. Nobody had any money. I was making $78 a month, which was pretty good money, but I was paying room and board and payments on a 1929 Model A Ford Coupe I had bought with my brother for $725. Thirty dollars to my dad and $35 for the car—that left me $13 a month to squander on myself. So I was broke.

"I wanted to learn how to fly but I didn't have any money, so I had to figure out how to get to fly, because I really wanted to be a pilot. I ended up going to the company. I got my nerve up—keep in mind I was a very shy kid, I wasn't one of these outgoing individuals who went out and made life for themselves, but when the chips were down I guess my stubborn streak would come out—so I ended up going in to the company and said, 'You've got a couple of Waco 10s out there you're not using. Can I borrow one?' They looked at me kinda funny and thought about it for a second or two and said, 'Well, you'd have to pay for the gas and oil.' I said, 'Well, okay, I can do that.' Gasoline was only nine cents a gallon. So I had an airplane. I ended up going to one of the captains, Chad Smith, and I said, 'Chad, I got an airplane. Would you teach me to fly?' And then he looked at me kinda funny and said, 'Sure, Joe, I'll do that.' So he soloed me. Took me six and a half hours to solo. I had a lot of airtime in the Ford. In the six to eight months I was a flight steward I got to sit up front with the captain every once in a while. They didn't have any autopilot, so he welcomed the opportunity to have someone spell him off. And they taught me how to fly the airplane in flight. Well, I got my license and soloed in September of 1930, and I built up my time and got my limited commercial license in November. Just about a month after I got my license, the Department of Commerce, which regulated aircraft in those days, came out with a new ruling requiring two pilots in aircraft weighing 12,500 pounds or more. That was just fit for the Ford Tri-Motor. So I just automatically became a copilot. Same job, same pay, but now I'm a pilot. This is unbelievable, but this is how aviation was in those days.

"I ended up flying a Hamilton and a Travel Air. I flew a couple flights when I was twenty-two years old as captain. Then the government came out with a new ruling that you had to be twenty-three years old and have an air transport rating, which required twelve hundred hours of flying time. I wasn't going to be twenty-three for about a month, until August, but after my birthday I went to Chicago and qualified and got my rating, came back at the end of the month in time to be told I was going to be flying as captain from Fargo to Grand Forks to Pembina.

"You can imagine the thrill of going out and being on your own and being captain and being on your own and flying your first captain flight, in a single-engine Hamilton. They had another captain up there, and between the two of us we covered everything. We were station manager in Fargo on one day, and the next day we were flying captain to Pembina and back, so we alternated that way. There was always one of us operating the station and one of us always flying. It was interesting because there was no radio aids or any of that kind of help. Clarence Bates was the name of the other pilot, and he happened to be a ham radio operator, and he had a ham station at home. And for some reason or other there was a radio in the Hamilton, so we used Clarence's home radio to keep in contact. If I were out for a flight, Clarence would call me and tell me what the weather was doing down in Fargo, and give me any information he thought I might need. I lived right next door to his home, so when he was flying up to Pembina I would go over to his house and give him a report on his radio."

On my end of the telephone, I tell Joe I am amazed. "Compared to today," I tell him, "this was the glory days of flying."

"It really was," he says. "You know, nobody knew anything about flying. There wasn't a single experienced pilot in the whole country. These guys that were flying were guys that after World War I bought surplus airplanes from the government for four hundred dollars and taught themselves to fly. And then to build up experience they would go around to small towns and give passenger rides, or they would go to the state fair and perform stunts like aerobatics or wing walking, even parachute jumping, anything to make a living. It was a carnival atmosphere. Nobody really had any experience; nobody really knew what they were doing. We had to learn as we went along."

"It's a wonder you guys didn't get lost!" I say.

"We got to know our routes," Joe says. "Every farm, every barn, every windmill. We could fly that way until the weather got down to about two hundred feet above the ground, and about a quarter of a mile visibility. When it got down to that we were not able to fly anymore, so wherever we were we would find a farmer's field, circle it to make sure there wasn't a haystack in the middle, and then land."

"What did your passengers think of that?" I ask.

"I'm sure they weren't very happy about being landed in the middle of a farmer's field, but that's the way it was. And you need to remember that the people who were flying were hardy people also. They were daring. They had as much courage as the pilot just to get into an airplane in those days. We would take them to town and put them on a train, and we would take the mail and put it on the train, and then we'd send a Western Union message back to St. Paul to let them know where we were. And we would stay there until the weather was good enough to fly again. Sometimes we would be there for two days!"

I ask if there are any stories that stick out in his mind more than others.

"You can't fly all the time I flew without having some episodes that are a little bit on the dicey side," he says. "I remember this one flight that was supposed to go to Chicago. The pilot was a man named Fred Livermore, who was a dapper young man. A natural-born pilot. When he sat in an airplane, that airplane became a part of him. He did amazing things with that Ford. He was also a daring type of individual. And remember we had to fly with visual reference to the ground at all times. Anyway, we got down to Winona, Minnesota, on the Mississippi River, and the weather popped down to practically nothing. We couldn't get any farther, so we turned around and decided to go back to Red Wing. When we got to Red Wing, we figured we'd go across the country and go down through Rochester, so we were coming in northwest of Rochester when the weather got really close. And for some reason or other he thought he could get out on top. He started climbing, and remember there were only a few instruments, and we climbed up through the overcast. When we got up to about five thousand feet, what happened was the Venturi tube on the outside of the aircraft iced up, so we lost our turn indicator. Then we stalled out. And when we stalled out we went into a dive and the engines would really hum, and then we'd pull back and the engines would get softer, but we'd stall out again. We finally broke out about two hundred feet above the ground and headed right for the trees, and he pulled that thing back as hard as he could. When we got back to St. Paul, they picked branches out of the landing gear."

"That's a great story," I tell him.

"You're never going to forget anything like that!" he says.

"How long did you fly?" I ask.

"Forty-two years, one month, and seventeen days. About thirty-six thousand hours."

There are more stories. Joe tells me about flying a way through the mountains with Amelia Earhart as a passenger, and about his last flight, coming back from Tokyo, flying a Boeing 707-320, how the tower operators in Seattle let his wife into the tower to give him final clearance to land. But I am thinking about thirty-six thousand hours of flying and what the turns of the planet must look like from that deep altitude.

. . .

At Pembina, North Dakota, the highway and the river are not very far apart. And as we follow the river, the airport simply appears in the distance, right under the nose of the airplane. It would be impossible not to see it. We're already lined up for a long final approach. We haven't found a thing. Not one barn top. No painted arrows or lights. But we have flown the route and looked. We have a story now, and that's worth everything.

When I land the Cessna, Joanna looks over at me.

"You have something against flaring?" she asks, smiling.

Ever the instructor, she points out that I've just made my second three-point landing in a tricycle-gear airplane. Just a little bit off, and that would be a good way to collapse the nose gear. It's been a year, and even though the plane feels familiar and good in my hands, there are things to remember and things to improve.

The runway pavement is broken and uneven. We taxi to the hangar and office and find the airport deserted. There are no planes on the ramp. No people in the office. The server is down for the computer that provides flight planning and weather information. Weeds grow around the metal rings in the ground for tie-downs. But the buildings are new; this whole place was underwater in 1997. A weathervane in the shape of a P-51 Mustang with a whirling propeller buzzes near the driveway. And just beyond it, a sight too good to be true.

An old metal light tower, exactly the type from the 1930s, rusted but upright, stands in the grass. An old beacon remains on top. It is not spinning, and I have no idea how long it's been dark. But there it is. At the end of the route, the light to welcome you home.

The Pilot's Journal

KBIS 181452Z 16005KT 10SM CLR 21/16
A3003 RMK AO2 SLP163 T02110156 58007

Our vessels consisted of six small canoes, and two large per-
ogues. This little fleet altho' not quite so rispectable as those
of Columbus or Capt. Cook were still viewed by us with as
much pleasure as those deservedly famed adventurers ever
beheld theirs; and I dare say with quite as much anxiety for
their safety and preservation. We were now about to pen-
etrate a country at least two thousand miles in width, on
which the foot of civilized man had never trodden; the good
or evil it had in store for us was for experiment yet to deter-
mine, and these little vessels contained every article by which
we were to expect to subsist or defend ourselves. However as this the state of mind in which we are, generally gives
the colouring to events, when the imagination is suffered to
wander into futurity, the picture which now presented itself
to me was a most pleasing one. Entertaining now as I do,

the most confident hope of succeeding in a voyage which had formed a darling project of mind for the last ten years of my life, I could but esteem this moment of our departure as among the most happy of my life.

—MERIWETHER LEWIS, Fort Mandan, April 7th, 1805

"Bismarck Tower, Cessna Five Three Two Nine Bravo is at one-three and ready to go, departing to the north, at or below three thousand, information Hotel."

"Cessna Five Three Two Nine Bravo, Bismarck Tower, wind one seven zero at eight, proceed on course, runway one-three, cleared for takeoff."

"Cleared for takeoff, Two Nine Bravo."

Here is something I believe. If I have said this before, forgive me. But there are two reasons for flying. The first is to get somewhere. To get somewhere fast. To get there directly. To haul you, your children, and your baggage to vacation or business. To haul a thousand troops with their vehicles and supplies. To haul relief food and shelter and medicine, parts of rocket ships, catalogs from department stores, to someplace where roads are not easy and time is important. This is hauling freight. This is transportation. This is where altitude and speed become the measures of efficiency.

But there is another reason, a better reason, a reason more closely aligned with beauty than utility, and this second reason has nothing to do with destination. It has nothing to do with efficiency. The second reason to fly is because you want to be airborne, to see the world from altitude, to once more get into a place where the large histories and relationships of geography, topography, meteorology, and sociology all blend into one complicated and beautiful landscape, the domain of

birds and angels. In the military, this is called aerial recon-
naissance. In a Cessna 152, this is called exploring.

> Capt. Clark walked on shore today, for several hours, when
> he returned he informed me that he had seen a gang of Ante-
> lopes in the plains but was unable to get a shoot at them he
> also saw some geese and swan. The geese are now feeding in
> considerable numbers on the young grass which has sprung
> up in the bottom praries—the Musquetoes were very trou-
> blesome to us today. The country on both sides of the Mis-
> souri from the tops of the river hills, is one continued level
> fertile plain as far as the eye can reach, in which there is not
> even a solitary tree or shrub to be seen except such as from
> their moist situations or the steep declivities of hills are shel-
> tered from the ravages of the fire.

> —MERIWETHER LEWIS, Wednesday April 10th, 1805

Quarter after ten in the morning, and I have just taken off
from Bismarck, North Dakota. The sky is clear; the grass
falling away beneath me is green. Passing two thousand feet
there are a couple of bumps, but nothing, nothing at all, to
be worried about. Just the air dancing on a summer morning. My plan is to head west, to the Missouri River, and then
turn north. My hope is to follow the river, past the fort where
Lewis and Clark spent their winter, the fort from which they
began the part of their trek that relied on imagination as
much as skill, until it reaches Garrison Dam, beyond which
the river becomes Lake Sakakawea, and then to follow that
for as long as my energies will last. I know, God willing, I
will land in Williston. If I fly straight and direct, Williston
is less than a two-hour flight. But I have four hours of fuel,
and my eyes are hungry. It is already a beautiful day.

West of the Missouri River, the shape and color of the land change fast. Buttes and hills. Hints of the Badlands beyond. Evidence that earth can move, can rise and fold, can be cut by water. Grasslands. East of the river, the land is flat and farmed. Small grains. Irrigated in places. East is green and black. West is brown and yellow.

At the river, sandbars line the sides and cut into the current. White-brown earth set against slate-blue water. At this low altitude, I can see the marks left by boats that have beached there and the tracks of people who have played. I make my turn to the north and look ahead instead of down. In the distance, the meandering river is silver with reflected light. Far away, the stacks of a power plant.

As Two Nine Bravo crosses the interstate, I can see Bismarck State College, the tower of the state capitol, traffic on city streets, traffic on I-94, traffic on the railway lines. I can see three golf courses and a marina. On the north side of town, a tank farm on the western banks. Hills and terraced fields. The neat order of planted windbreaks. To the west, the neighboring town of Mandan. Ahead, pontoon boats tied up at docks along the river shore.

On the radio I hear other traffic leaving the airport. Then suddenly there are kayaks on the river. Yellow, blue, two red, another blue. No one is paddling. They all drift and talk— a scene of getting ready. A woman in a red kayak looks up at the sound of my engine and waves. I rock the wings, and then they all wave. All of us, perhaps, river explorers today. Then a houseboat tied up at a sandbar.

Is it *possible* to explore from the air?

I have always thought that at its very core, exploration is an intimate act. It requires a kind of closeness. The ability to touch, to see, to taste and hear and smell. It requires that you actually *be* someplace. In other words, to explore a river you need to be in, or at least on, that river. Yet we also understand that the word is larger. It is possible to explore an idea, a feeling, a damn good question. But even here, don't you need to be present in that moment? Can you explore at a distance? Can you explore in the abstract? There is a part of me that wants to say no, absolutely not. An explorer has dirty boots and worn laces. But what about those who explore with microscopes, with telescopes, with differential equations and algorithms, with chemical bonds, with new combinations of chord and harmony? There is a part of me that wants to say yes, absolutely yes.

I am three thousand feet in the air. I can see the river, its light and dark colors where it is shallow and deep. I can see how stuck logs create their own sandbars, and follow the arcing line of sand trailing underwater down-current from the obstruction. I can see the rows of homes, each with their own dock, on the west side of the river. And I can see the tractor in the field several miles from the water. What's more—I can see all of this at the same time. What I can see is the way things set up next to each other. If the explorer's real question is "What is the relationship between *here* and *not here*?" then perhaps the airship is the first best way toward an answer.

There is a bend in the river, a sweeping left and then a right and then another left. If I were flying to get somewhere, I would cut across it, take the direct route. But this is not a day for directness. I am touring. I am wandering. Perhaps I am exploring, too. I want to see things I have never seen, and see them in a way my imagination can only imagine.

A little crosswind hits the plane. A little tailwind pushes me along. Two Nine Bravo and I settle over the water, three thousand feet above sea level, one thousand three hundred and fifty feet, more or less, above the river. A check of the gauges and everything looks good. If I knew this river and the air above it, I would fly even lower. I would slide into the space not very far above the water and fly the river course between the riparian trees. Hard banks in the airplane when there are hard banks in the shore. The thrill of flying the river's shape on a summer morning. But I have never been here before. I do not want to meet an unexpected bridge or power line with the front end of an airplane.

Off in the distance, north and west, a forest of wind towers. White spires rising from brown and green earth. Long white blades turning with such measured grace the only word I can think of is *elegant*. It would be easy to say they look like windmills, but that would not be entirely true. A windmill is the first draft. This is the anniversary edition. Much like the distance between the Stanley Steamer and the Porsche, it's tough to see the connection beyond the most basic four tires on the ground and forward motion.

The river bends, widens, and the sandbars become more pronounced. I wonder what you would have imagined two hundred years ago, wandering away from the river toward the buttes and grasslands, nothing but buffalo and endless prairie. Already just this little bit north of Bismarck the homes have disappeared. The pleasure traffic on the river has disappeared. No kayaks. No pontoons. Cropland to the east.

Grassland to the west. A long train filled with coal cars on the west side of the river.

Fluid sky and fluid river. Huge coal-fired power plants. Coal mines, too. Huge planet-cutting shovels digging what looks like canals or opening veins in the earth. Wind farms. Then grassland and crops bending in the breeze. Even though I live in Minnesota, my town is a border town and North Dakota is home territory, perhaps even more close to my heart because my imagination turns much more often west than east. So there is a sense of history with the sense of place. I half expect to see buffalo. Not just one or two, or even a dozen, but the massive herds from the history of the plains. Herds that counted into the tens of thousands. When the people become sparse, as they do quickly here, it's the buffalo that fills the spaces. Sometimes the real animal. Sometimes just the idea. I don't know if I would recognize one from three thousand feet, but my heart tells me that there should be buffalo.

An old gray abandoned farmstead sits in a field on the west side of the river, the walls and roof leaning south, away from the usual wind.

Soft cotton-ball clouds. Brown, green, yellow earth. Beautiful day. More hills and rises, gentle folds. Ahead of me I can see what looks like the beginning of Badlands. Bluffs along the river's edge. And then Garrison Dam, low and broad like the plains, the fifth-largest earthen dam in the world, the waters of the Missouri pooled behind it to become Lake Sakakawea. Bright-silver surge tanks at the gates. A concrete spillway on the eastern side so large I could land this airplane more easily there than at the small airstrip that parallels the foot of the earthen wall.

Left and right over the river, then crossing the dam, each moment carries me and Two Nine Bravo farther away from shore. Thinking about glide slope for a moment—the pilot's habit of wondering where to land if landing needs to be quick—I note the point where it becomes more likely I would be swimming instead of walking away from an unexpected need to get down. And I will admit I smile.

I see only one powerboat and one sailboat out on the lake. I don't know what people on the ground will think of seeing me fly by, banking left and right over the river and then over them, but I hope they think it's a pretty sight.

There is no such thing as a trail in the air. No pathway to follow, carved into any hillside or marked with the boot prints of those before you. Unlike other trails, the air is always fresh when you meet it, and vanished the moment you cross it. While there are these things called Victor airways, they are navigational fictions. Compass headings and radio beams. They exist only in the electronic and say nothing of the physical world. Mountain trails remain where they are, slowly eroding perhaps, but stable enough for the span of a human lifetime. Waterways change slowly, but generally not within a generation.

The air changes by the moment, each bit of weather and wind, starlight and storm, making this place, if *place* is the right word, nothing like it has ever been before or will ever be again. My flight today is easy. Clear air, smooth air, white birds below me. Cranes or egrets, I don't know. Not a soul on the radio. Very nice bluffs along the lakeshore. Almost the sensation of heading out over open water, what it must be like to head out over an ocean. Looking down to see different colors on and in the water, different colors in the waves.

With the bright sun, I know this afternoon the air will turn to thermals, the hot columns of rising air that make for rock-and-roll flying. And tomorrow there will be storms. Tomorrow there will be hard wind. In months ahead there will be tornado and blizzard. History, my own history here, tells me these things are true. I could fly this route every day and never fly the same air twice.

Over toward the north shore here, eroded bluffs and buttes make towers and freestanding pinnacles in the water. Almost like Acadia National Park on the Atlantic shore in Maine, except here it's the brown earth of the prairie instead of the black rock of New England. These will be here tomorrow, even though the air that would bring me to them will change.

> The wind was in our favour after 9 A.M. and continued favourable until 3 P.M. we therefore hoisted both the sails in the White Perogue, consisting of a small squar sail, and spritsail, which carried her at a pretty good gate, until about 2 in the afternoon when a suddon squall of wind struck us and turned the perogue so much on the side as to alarm Sharbono who was steering at the time, in this state of alarm he threw the perogue with her side to the wind, when the spritsail gibing was as near overseting the perogue as it was possible to have missed.
>
> —MERIWETHER LEWIS, Saturday April 13th, 1805

From altitude, of course, you can see underwater a little bit. You can see rises in the lake bottom, where little peninsulas continue under the surface. Like looking at a picture of the

Caribbean in *National Geographic.* The red soil and brown turning to green and blue underwater.

Of course, Lewis and Clark saw nothing like this.

I pass a group of one, two, three, four, five-six-seven-eight small boats all clustered around the same point. I can't see if anyone is in the water swimming. A short while later, two more boats filled with fishermen. Other boats now speed up and down the lake, darting out of one cover to tuck into the next one. Then several boats all together pretty far up in a northern sidewater—fishermen all looking for their special spot.

Cloud shadows on the water, and riffles from the wind, make patterns on the surface: seagulls and rocking horses, dragons and lightning.

A turn is coming. North this time. The land on the southern side of the lake gets pronouncedly more wrinkled, the beginnings of the Badlands of everyone's imagination, softly at first, then some weathered tops, then some deeper ravines. Finally the cuts and divides and valleys and rises of the picture postcards.

Flying right down the middle of the lake, a thousand feet above the surface, both shores and the lake for miles in front of me all a part of the *here*, the easy bank of the wings as the lake makes its turns past the entrance of the Little Missouri River, I am as happy as any explorer whose new lands are gentle and shining under favorable skies.

We saw also many tracks of the white [plains grizzly] bear of enormous size, along the river shore and about the carcases of the Buffaloe, on which I presume they feed. We have not as yet seen one of these anamals, tho' their tracks are so abundant and recent. The men as well as ourselves are anxious to meet with some of these bear. the Indians give a very formidable account of the strengh and ferocity of this animal, which they never dare to attack but in parties of six eight or ten persons; and are even then frequently defeated with the loss of one or more of their party.

—MERIWETHER LEWIS, Saturday April 13th, 1805

A white sailboat on the lake, beautiful on the dark blue of the water under cloud shadows. If this were the ocean, you'd see rollers and breakers coming up on the beach. But here, today, there is nothing of the sort. This is the American prairie in a very good mood. What waves there are seem meant only for entertainment, the necessary beauty of large water.

I approach the next turn, this one left, to the west, the start of the stretch that will take me to Williston and the landing there, and spend a little time flying slowly over the two islands in the way. The first one, the southernmost, small and round, is the kind of place where in your imagination you could put a home, if you wanted to own your own island. Some trees. Some open space. Blue water all around. It's just the right size. And then just north of it, an island much longer as measured from east to west, and much narrower measured north to south. A crescent moon of an island. Like Sable Island, in the North Atlantic. A place for storms and wild horses.

As I come up to the left turn, it's easy to look at the landscape around here and imagine that it's all virgin—that nobody has been here. There is another old gray weathered farmstead sitting out near the south point just where the lake turns, and yes there is a town in the distance, and yes

I can see another town in the farther distance on the other side, and if I scan the far horizon I can see grain elevators and towers and the reflective roofs of a thousand buildings, but right here along the lake it's easy to believe this is what it once was, even though the lake was never here. Buffalo. Dire Wolf. Plains Grizzly. Mastodon.

> The broken hills of the Missouri about this place exhibit large irregular and broken masses of rocks and stones; some of which tho' 200 feet above the level of the water at some former period to have felt it's influence, for they appear smoth as if woarn by the agitation of the water. . . . I ascended to the top of the cutt bluff this morning, from whence I had a most delightfull view of the country, the whole of which except the vally formed by the Missouri is void of timber or underbrush, exposing to the first glance of the spectator immence herds of Buffaloe, Elk, deer, & Antelopes feeding in one common and boundless pasture.

—MERIWETHER LEWIS, Monday April 22nd, 1805

My Lord, this is beautiful. Sakakawea makes a turn to the west, and just after that the shore turns to serious Badlands. Even though I know I'm higher, it looks like the buttes in front of me are in my way. Three white egrets or cranes, black-tipped white wings, fly below me on the left. Beautiful sight! The air is beginning to roil a bit, enough heating from the sun to make the thermals start and the air dance. Small bumps lift the airplane, shake and rattle the wingtips. I can see oil wells, the up and down and revolving motion of the wellhead pumps.

This airplane, this sky, this earth below me, my own hand on the yoke and feet on the pedals, they have all found the cadence and tempo of each other, and for a short while there is nothing but this airplane, this sky, this earth below me and my own body above. My friend Marvin, a poet, once told me about a scholar who used the world *flow* to describe the absence of time when the reading gets really good—when suddenly it's three in the morning and you don't remember seeing two or one or even 9:35. In an e-mail he writes, "The Hungarian/Transylvanian-born psychologist Mihaly Csikszentmihalyi writes of a feeling he calls 'flow.' The flow he means is the state we enter—he also calls it 'optimal experience'—when we are so totally involved in what we are doing that we lose track of time. We feel serene, sometimes ecstatic. We have a sense of clarity. We transcend our egos. Whatever we are doing, doing it is its own reward." And that's exactly how I feel as the Badlands meet the river and Two Nine Bravo skims the midmorning sky. Everything else be damned. I could do this forever.

Then again, there comes a time when a pilot's mind turns to landing. No matter how beautiful the sky, how magical the shape of the water, how deep the wandering and wondering might be, there is that moment when your hands and feet and eyes and mind all turn to one choreography and one desire. To bring this ship safely into port. To bring this airship down so nicely the tires just kiss the ground and then weight takes over, where lift goes away and all is well. And for me, this morning, that time is now.

I can see some haze in the distance. There will be thunderstorms here later tonight, great big soul dumpings from the western sky. Lightning too, which from other storms could set the whole prairie on fire. But tonight the forecast says there will be an old-fashioned thumper of a downpour with timpani.

Long before these storms move over the Missouri, however, Two Nine Bravo and I will be hundreds of miles away, heading back toward Fargo. But now, the river and willows underneath my wheels and the town of Williston plainly ahead, there is nothing but blue sky and blue lake. Cotton-ball clouds. Green and brown earth. And a little Cessna 152.

The GPS says I'm not very far away when the radio comes to life.

"Williston Traffic, Cessna Four Four Zero One Bravo, departing on one-one, southeast bound, Williston Traffic."

"Williston Traffic," I reply. "Cessna Five Three Two Nine Bravo is nineteen miles out to the southeast, setting up for a right traffic downwind, Williston."

"Williston Traffic, Cessna Four Four Zero One Bravo is just off one-one and departing the area to the southeast, Williston."

"Two Nine Bravo is approaching from the southeast, thirty-seven hundred feet."

"Roger, I'll level off at three thousand for now."

"Very good."

I would like to watch the river. Suddenly very shallow and breaking into a hundred meandering braids—how would a river pilot ever know which course to take?—the water is crowded with light- and dark-green willow trees from shore to shore. I would like to watch the way the colors under the water change and the way the sunlight reflects from the water and adds a backlight highlight to the river-shore bluffs. But now there is an airplane somewhere in front of me, heading toward me, and I cannot see it.

"Cessna Four Four Zero One Bravo is five southeast of the Williston airport and level at three thousand."

"Cessna Five Three Two Nine Bravo is fifteen southeast of Williston, level at thirty-seven hundred."

Moments pass. I keep looking forward, trying to spot the reflected glint of metal at altitude in the sunshine. Nothing.

"Williston Traffic, Five Three Two Nine Bravo is ten southeast of the Williston airport at thirty-seven hundred feet."

"Zero One Bravo is also ten southeast, three thousand feet. We don't see you, but that's okay."

I look around and over each shoulder. I should have seen this airplane, and he should have seen me. But we are safely past each other now, each of us happy in the open sky.

"Williston Traffic, Cessna Five Three Two Nine Bravo is entering a long downwind for runway one-one, right traffic, Williston."

I watch the town grow near and smile when the straight line of the runway is clear and bright. Safe haven. A good port. The idea is the same through the centuries.

"Williston Traffic, Cessna Five Three Two Nine Bravo is downwind right traffic, runway one-one, Williston."

But then, "Williston Traffic, Cherokee Six Gulf Bravo Whiskey Whiskey is on the ramp, going to taxi to the approach end of runway one-one."

I see the plane on the ground, just starting to roll. He will wait for me.

"Williston Traffic, Cessna Five Three Two Nine Bravo is turning base."

Hang around the back end of airports for a while and you'll start to see pictures that all look pretty much the same—a runway about a half mile ahead and about a thousand feet below. This is short final, the part of the approach when you commit or you don't. This is the spot when you know if you're set up right or if you need to think really fast. Pilots take pictures of these approaches, to say where they have been, and to remind themselves what those moments held. Almost like pictures of infant children, they all look pretty much the same until it's one of yours. You don't see it in the photograph, but for the pilot that picture holds the whole airplane, the wind ahead or cross, the sound of the engine, the feel of the rudder against the feet.

"Williston Traffic, Cessna Five Three Two Nine Bravo is turning final."

When I finish the turn and raise the wing, the picture is not right. For whatever reason, despite the altimeter that says I'm right where I should be, my eyes tell me I am just a little too high. Or just a little too close for the altitude. In any case, I have to do something. I could turn a slow descending circle and bleed off the vertical distance that way. I could do what's called a slip, a way to make the airplane awkward in the sky, and watch the runway until I like where I am. Or I could have a bit of fun. With the throttle already all the way back, I just push the nose down and fly a bit more directly toward the ground. And then pull back when it's time.

"Williston Traffic, Two Nine Bravo is on the ground, runway one-one."

After I had completed my observations in the evening I walked down and joined the party at their encampment on the point of land fromed by the junction of the rivers; found them all in good health, and much pleased at having arrived at this long wished for spot, and in order to add in some measure to the general pleasure which seemed to pervade our little community, we ordered a dram to be issued to each person; this soon produced the fiddle, and they spent the evening with much hilarity, singing & dancing, and seemed as perfectly to forget their past toils, as they appeared regardless of those to come.

—MERIWETHER LEWIS, Friday April 26th, 1805

Altitude

Thirty-six thousand feet over central Montana on a clear, bright summer morning, I am sitting in an exit-row window seat on a Northwest Airlines flight from Minneapolis to Portland, Oregon. The airplane is full. Businessmen and -women. One or two families with children in tow. A number of people clearly heading for adventures with hiking boots or kayaks. A thousand bags stuffed into overhead compartments.

The couple in the center and aisle seats next to me, somewhere in their late twenties and flirting, lean toward each other to talk, as considerate to me as they are interested in each other, and the flight attendants are making their second passes down the aisle. Refills of coffee and soda. It's a pleasant flight, in the way that commercial flights attempt to make the entire process invisible, or at least forgettable, and everyone seems comfortable if not happy.

I am bothered, though, by my window. It could not be more badly placed. Just above my left knee, and too far forward for any casual or consistent viewing, I have to strain forward and bend over to see anything at all. And when I do, I'm aware that I'm blocking the view for everyone else in the row. But even the Sirens would pale next to the call of an airplane window, so bend and strain I do, repeatedly.

Montana is a state I know on the ground. Behind the wheel of a Jeep I have crossed the passes and the highways and back roads for years. Beartooth Pass. Traveler's Rest. The Highline. A thousand small roads, paved and dirt, between one place and another. There are rivers I know just off the roads where the trout have been willing, and there are cafés I know where the portions have been the size of the state. When I lean forward to look out the airplane window, my second cup of coffee cooling in my hand, I expect the familiar drama of mountains and sky, but I do not expect anything new.

For just a moment, I simply scan the area below the plane. Interstate highway. I-90. Not much traffic. Brown springtime earth. But the mountains on the south side of the highway give way to a valley after a small opening to let a river out. Wait, I think. That's Livingston! So that would be the Yellowstone River. That would be Paradise Valley. Yes, in the distance there, glimmering and bright, Yellowstone Lake! Yes, oh Lord, in the distance, a small group of peaks that rise well above the others—those are the Tetons! I can see it all as one grand, sweeping, wonderful sight. There is no cloud in the sky. No haze. Nothing at all to make the view anything less than breath-stealing and spectacular. Flatlands and mountains. Snow-topped peaks. Intensely blue water. I know all these places. But I have never seen them together. In my mind they are hours and miles and worlds of energies apart.

There is narrative in landscape, and so my eye follows the Yellowstone River south from Livingston, through the narrow pass and up the valley. So very pretty, I think. And when I can no longer see the river, my eye settles on the lake for a moment, and in the back of my head my memories, both personal and academic, find their voices. There are rocks in Yellowstone that are fifty million years old, or older. And, oddly, there are rocks that are only half a million years old, if not very much fresher. This difference is the remains of a disaster. This is the basin of a tremendous caldera, thirty-four miles across in one direction, forty-five miles across in the other, site of the one of the planet's largest volcanic eruptions. A supervolcano. The remains of the explosion have been found in California, Saskatchewan, Wyoming, Nebraska, Iowa, the Gulf of Mexico, and beyond. Not so much a fault line as perhaps a migrating subterranean hot spot, there is magma below these mountains and it's still churning hot. Water seeping down to the heat makes the geysers and hot springs. Dozens of ancient lava flows make up the layers in the earth. The lake bed has been rising and falling recently, and on television the science programs often wonder what would happen if it were to blow again. The answer is not good. But there are also memories of sunrise and sunset, fish that rose to a fly and the sound of wolves at night, the strange peace that comes from knowing you are very far away from anyone else.

Farther south, my eye lingers on the Tetons. And from somewhere I remember that this is sedimentary rock, now schist and gneiss, lifted from an ancient sea, with magma intrusions and glacial carving. From somewhere else I remember that every footfall on the ground there is thrilling.

Personal memories and bits of book learning notwithstanding, what I cannot get over is seeing all of it at the same time. To see that each of these places and each of these stories rest in the shadow of the others. It's a humbling moment when connections and dependencies and relationships are made obvious and clear. No part of the earth is disconnected from any other. This is the lesson of the photographs sent back from the Apollo missions. One earth. One round gem in the dark of the universe. This is the lesson of the songlines in Australia, too. Looking out this airplane window, I can see—and sight is as intimate and physical as touch—that my stories in one place have everything to do with my stories next door. More often than not, I'm just too ignorant to hear.

To be honest, though, I've had this feeling and this insight a thousand times. Every time it's as fresh and as rattling as the first, but still it's something I'm coming to know. It is the particular and peculiar grace of altitude.

There is a large map hanging on the wall over my desk at the college. Bright-white paper stock, a jet-black frame, made by the Raven Map and Image Company, it is a picture of North America, from the Gulf of Panama to the tip of Ellesmere Island, from Barbados to Attu in the Near Islands of Alaska. And it is, in a word, beautiful. This map is art. As stunning as any drawing from the Middle Ages, as provoking as the lines in the journals of Lewis and Clark. Infinitely more complex than either. Shades for elevation. Names for people-places and geography. Roadways and borders. The closer your nose gets to the map, the more detail comes clear. The farther away, the more the whole dance seems to be made.

In my chair in front of my desk, this is a map for dreaming, for lingering, for wondering how one place fits up against someplace else. There is the circle of the Manicouagan impact

crater in Quebec. There is the Mississippi River delta. There
is the terminal moraine we've come to call Long Island. And
there is the crescent of the Snake River plain in Idaho. In my
chair, head tilted back, I have spent hours fitting what few
stories I know to the image on my wall. Something from
outer space pounds a hole in Quebec. A glacier pushes dirt
into a long pile for the New York wealthy. Another glacier
suddenly gives way and drains all of Lake Bonneville down
the Snake River plain. These are the easy ones. But I have
also spent hours, many more hours, just looking, trying to
imagine how things came to look like this, trying to hear
whatever echoes there may be of old stories before people.
Looking at the map, which is exactly like looking at a story,
I have imagined a million histories, none of them valid, all
of them possible. Landscape is always an invitation to curiosity and desire.

One day, and I have no good memory of why, I leaned
forward enough to read the map's credits. "Map produced
by Allan Cartography of Medford, Oregon, with the assis-
tance of Dr. A. Jon Kimerling, Department of Geoscienc-
es, Oregon State University." I leaned back again, suddenly
filled with the obvious question. A minute later, the e-mail
went out.

Hi Jon,

Quick left field question. I'm working on a book about
flying, and in my office I have the large North American
map you did for Raven maps. Can you tell me about what
altitude that view would be from?

Thanks,
W. Scott Olsen

Not even two hours later, I had a reply.

Subject: Re: Raven map question

Scott, This is a very good question that I have never been asked before. First of all, the altitude must depend on the map viewing distance. Say you are viewing the map from 3 feet away. The North America map is at a scale of 1:9,000,000 at its center, which is about 150 miles to the inch. One inch on the map will subtend an angle in radians of $2*\tan(1/36)$ at this viewing distance. This same angle will be maintained if the 36 to 1 ratio of viewing distance to map distance is kept, so the viewing distance (altitude) would be 36 times 150 miles, or about 5400 miles above the surface.

Hope this helps. Jon.

Something about imagining my head fifty-four hundred miles above the surface of the earth while sitting in a mostly comfortable office made me smile. So I wrote back immediately.

Jon,

Perfect!

Hell of a map, by the way. Thank you.

Scott

And he wrote back, too.

Subject: Re: Raven map question

Scott, Thanks. This seems a reasonable explanation to me, but I hope that this is in fact true.

Jon.

And then a few moments later:

Scott, I just realized that in defining the subtended angle
that must be maintained, I used the full distance and
not the half distance that should be used in the tangent
equation. The equation should read $2 \tan(0.5/360)$. This
equation only defines the subtended angle and does not
affect the altitude value of 5400 miles obtained by a
proportion.

Jon.

Good enough, I thought. Even though I have no idea what a
subtended angle might be. Such care in the science. Such wonder in the mind. Fifty-four hundred miles above the earth, it's
possible to forget everything that nags at daily life. No mort-
gages. No insurance worries. No electric bills. No city coun-
cil votes. Fifty-four hundred miles above the earth and suddenly, I understand, what is left is just the earth, the whole
of it all, the hard physical beauty of the planet, and the desire to have it make sense. This is the grace of altitude.

There is nothing about any of this in the flight manuals,
but perhaps there should be. Every pilot—and I mean every pilot—will tell you the same thing. Once you get off the
ground just a few hundred feet, the planet changes. I don't
mean the rush of takeoff, the thrill when you feel in your
body the moment the wheels leave the ground and you are
holding a machine in your hands that can move in three di-
mensions, that can turn you upside down or roll you over
and then point toward heaven. I mean the quieter feeling
just a few moments later, when you can see the next town,
when you can see the river in the distance, when the horizon
is a 360-degree circle around you, when you can see a rain
cloud twenty miles away and the sun on wheat fields below

you, and you can see all of this at the same time. You begin to understand new connections.

Some people call this perspective or the aerial view. But to me, the word that has always seemed best is a complicated term. A few hundred feet off the ground and you begin to understand *grace*.

If you ask a religious person, he or she will tell you that grace is a gift from God, unearned yet often unused, and this gift is what allows humans to act righteously. Grace is what we need to get beyond our base behaviors and limitations. Grace is required for a kind of moral evolution and in some ways the passport we present at the pearly gates. If you ask a classical historian, you will learn that there were three Graces, goddesses of charm and beauty and creativity, and that together they were called the Charities. If you ask a dancer, you will learn that grace is a kind of fluidity in motion. If you ask a parent of small children, you will be reminded that grace is a prayer of thanksgiving said before a meal.

As the airplane climbs beyond five hundred feet or so above the ground, you begin to understand that every single one of these ideas is true at the very same time.

I am no theologian. But I am told that in the early centuries of the Christian church, in the early days of the monastic movement, there was an idea that the *first* step toward understanding God's grace was to get rid of your passions. In this sense, passions meant your involvement in the mundane, the arguments about daily life, whether your cousin was going to be elected to the school board. This is why monasteries are so often in the wilderness. Distance provides perspective. Perspective allows for a new way of seeing how the world is arranged.

It would be possible to argue that a pilot is very much like a monk, alone in his cell, contemplating the universe, knowing that every action has meaning.

Or maybe the best way to think about this is entirely opposite. I would like to believe the pilot shares something deep with the archaeologist. The archaeologist is neither biologist nor cartographer, though he is familiar with both and uses those insights to begin his own. The archaeologist looks at the land, tries to discern where humans would have done something, then digs and uncovers and excavates to discover if in fact they did. If evidence is found, the real questions begin. What is this thing, this shard, this tool? How was it used? What does it tell us about the people who once lived or walked or used this place? How are the patterns of our life related to theirs? What can their echoes teach us?

A thousand feet above the ground, it seems to me the same type of uncovering is possible. Instead of removing soil and rock to let air onto some foundation or grave, however, what the pilot removes is the limited scope of the human eye. Roads extend to the horizon. The marks where roads used to be remain fresh on the earth. The way one place needs another is suddenly evident in the pathways, the pipelines, the power lines, the rivers and canals. The way one place is kept separate from another is revealed in the height of a ridge or the depth of a valley, the width of a lake. No place is without relation to some other place. Perhaps the archaeologist is the micro-observer, inferring the character of a people from a shard of pottery, while the pilot is the macro-observer, learning the same truths from the relations made real on the land.

But then I have an e-mail from my friend Doug Burton-Christie, who *is* a theologian.

Scott,

Theological observations: both grace and the "passions" are deep and complex ideas in Christianity. Nothing you have said about either is inaccurate. But I would add a couple of thoughts.

1. Grace, for a thinker like Augustine, is the very ground of our existence, without which life is unimaginable. Our ability to imagine God, to love, to reach conscious awareness of our life, to pray—these are all deeply graced reality. There is nothing apart from grace. It is primordial.

2. The passions. The master of this whole area of thought is a monk called Evagrius. You can read in his work Praktikos a phenomenological account of the "eight principal passions" (later the seven deadly sins). For Evagrius and the other early Xian monks, passions (not at all to be identified with what we mean when we say someone is passionate about something) represent a way of thinking and talking about those places in our lives where we are "caught," "compromised," "unfree." Overcoming the passions (Evagrius believed it was possible to experience a state of "apatheia"—an existence free of the passions) was inextricably bound up with the process through which one is reborn, made free. Attending to the passions was for the monks a crucial part of ascetic practice, which was also bound up with coming to "know the self."

Hope this is not too obscure . . .

Doug

Could I get away with this? Could I claim that the real magic of altitude was somehow a mixture of the perspective of an archaeologist and the vision of second-century monks? Flying is hardly ascetic, but yes. Absolutely. Yes.

Back in the Northwest Airlines jet, I had a question. I knew our altitude was 36,000 feet. Given that, how far could I see? At that height, how far away is the horizon? What was the limit, here, of the connections I could imagine? When we landed, another quick e-mail to Jon, and then his reply to look at a Web site. The math was easy.

D = 112.88 km v (h). That is, distance equals 112.88 kilometers times the square root of the height of the observer, expressed in kilometers.

So:

Airplane: 36,000 feet above sea level.

Livingston airport (Mission Field): 4,660 feet above sea level.

Height of airplane over ground: 31,340 feet.

31,340 feet equals 9,552 meters.

9,552 meters equals 9.552 kilometers.

So, D = 112.88 times the square root of 9.552.

Distance equals 349 kilometers, or 216 miles.

I know from the charts that the distance from Mission Field to the top of Grand Teton is 136 miles. So 80 miles beyond that peak, the ground falls away from my view. In every direction, 216 miles. If 216 is the radius and pi times the radius squared is the area of a circle, then from this airplane I can see 146,499.84 square miles of this planet. Every inch of it connected to every other. Every connection inviting an explanation of the relationship. And if I am hungry, all I need to do is go up.

A Prairie Roll

KFAR 031653Z 18013KT 10SM CLR 01/M03
A2954 RMK AO2 SLP014 T00061028

Conditions at: KFAR (FARGO, ND, US) observed 1653 UTC
03 January 2007

Temperature: 0.6°C (33°F)

Dew point: -2.8°C (27°F) [RH = 78%]

Pressure (altimeter): 29.54 inches Hg (1000.4 mb)

[Sea-level pressure: 1001.4 mb]

Winds: from the S (180 degrees) at 15 mph (13 knots;
6.8 m/s)

Visibility: 10 or more miles (16+ km)

Ceiling: at least 12,000 feet AGL

Clouds: sky clear below 12,000 feet AGL

Weather: no significant weather observed at this time

I do not want to climb Mount Everest. It would be interesting, I think, to be on the summit for a moment, for only the view it must provide, everything on earth below the five feet and ten inches I would add to the highest point, but there is nothing in me that compels me toward this climb. No itch appears in my spirit that says I must face this challenge or reach this point for my life to be complete and whole. I admire the men and women who do climb that hill, tremendously, and if I have not read every book about that place, then I have read nearly every one. But I have read their stories, contentedly, a cup of coffee in my hand, a collie named Chaucer curled up at my feet.

So how is it also true that everything in me urges me to that mountain? How is it true that deep down I know I will do whatever it takes before I am pushing a walker down some antiseptic hallway to be at the base of what is called Chomolungma, Goddess Mother of the World, in Tibet, and Sagarmatha, Goddess of the Sky, in Nepal? Not to climb. Just to be there. To see the thing. To witness the snow plume blowing off the summit in real life and not in photo paper or pixels. To pick up a rock from this place and hold it in my hand. To trek in from the airstrip in Lukla, stroll around the village of Namche Bazar, kick dirt and snow from my boots as I set up a tent at 17,998 feet above sea level. To say to myself and others that I have been there, and seen the place, and tasted its air.

Likewise, I grew up in the television shadow of Jacques Cousteau and Lloyd Bridges. I read the adventures of the *Nautilus*, both the Jules Verne version and the atomic-powered one that crossed under the North Pole, a thousand times. Every magazine article on undersea archaeology grew tattered in my possession. Every picture of some undersea habitat had me wondering where I would fit. And I sat, rapt, in front of that silly TV show with the flying minisub. Yet

I also knew the full life leap underwater was not, for me, necessary. And I knew, at the very same time, there was no way to keep a tank off my back. When those chances come, I take every one.

Think about the phrase "Just once." We use it every day. Just once, we say, I'd like to play at Carnegie Hall. Just once, I'd like to win the lottery. Just once, I'd like to take a fast lap around the Indianapolis Motor Speedway. Just once, I'd like to see what it feels like to touch my dream.

What does any of this have to do with flying? It's simple. Like nearly everyone else, I have stood slack jawed and amazed at air shows, watching aerobatics. Loops and rolls and stalls of a dozen shapes and styles. Maneuvers I cannot imagine how to get into much less get out of. The inside loop. The outside loop. The Immelmann. The Cuban Eight. The Hammerhead Stall. Rolling Circles. Countless ways to make these moves unique. The Half This or the Reverse That. A hundred ways to find an edge in the sky. And standing at those air show fields I know two things simultaneously. I know I will never be a competition aerobatic pilot. My hours will go to an entirely different aesthetic. The grace and beauty of the air, for me, is not in the precision of some line. But I also know I have to try, at least one move, at least one time.

Just west and a little bit north of Fargo, North Dakota's Hector International Airport, Jake Gust and his wife, Barb Olive, farm four hundred acres of wheat, soybeans, and corn. I've known them both for more than twenty years. Barb is a professor emerita from the English Department where I teach, and the office I sit in was once hers. Jake, an engineer by education, specializing in product development, also manages a city water-diversion project. But more important, Jake is a pilot. He started flying in 1958, flew for the air force out of Waco, Texas, on board a refueling tanker, and for many years he flew spray planes up and down the Red River valley, on the border of Minnesota and North Dakota. Jake's son, David, became a spray-plane pilot, too. But these days, Jake is an *aerobatic* pilot.

"Jake," I said on the phone one day, sheepishly, "I want to learn how to fly just one trick. Just once. I really don't want to take aerobatic lessons. I really don't want to compete at all. But there's no way I'm going to call myself a pilot if I haven't learned even the simplest stunt."

He knew I was fishing for an invitation. "What do you want to learn?" he asked me.

There was a small part of me that wanted to ask for something wild, difficult, complicated, and extreme. Something that would put a "No way!" look on the faces of the pilots I know. But the larger part of me wanted just that one simple move that seems to be a celebration in the air, the one move that seems to be an act of joy and grace, and is simply so damn pretty to see in the air your heart nearly leaps after the plane.

"Jake," I said, "I want to learn how to fly a roll."

Sometimes you hear a story and you nod your head, thinking, Okay, I get it. Nothing special. Just good information. And then some other detail comes along and that story is exploded, everything you imagined the first time shattered, and your mind works overtime to reassemble the old parts with the new. First you learn that Beethoven wrote symphonies.

Then you learn about the concertos. Sometime later you learn he was deaf. George Dawson, you learn, explored Canada in the 1870s the way Lewis and Clark explored America. One of the greats, you learn, in surveying and natural history. And later you learn he had Pott's disease, a tuberculosis of the spine that left him with a curved back and a body no bigger than a twelve-year-old boy. The new details don't match your first imagination, but then they find a way to fit, and you smile when you discover your imagination is larger and more richly detailed.

I am thinking about this late at night, a howling January wind shaking the ash, maple, spruce, and apple trees in my backyard, because I have been trying to answer what I thought would be a simple question. Who flew the first roll? The Web was no help. Searching the college library and the databases gave me nothing at all. Only this morning I called an aerobatic association, and the woman on the phone didn't know. But she had me get in touch with a man named Mike Heuer, the president of the Fédération Aéronautique Internationale's Aerobatics Commission. "If anyone will know," she said, "he will." She gave me his phone number, and I called straightaway. He answered on the first ring.

"You know," he said, after I'd asked my question, "I don't know! Let me do some research and get back to you."

We traded e-mail addresses and said good-bye. Already this evening, my computer beeped to announce new mail.

Sir,

Good talking to you today.

I learned something today I didn't know.

The first recorded "slow roll" (which is really what you

are looking for) was done by Maurice Chevillard on 6
November 1913 in a Henri Farman biplane (powered by
an 80 hp Gnome) at Juvisy, France.

My best,

Mike Heuer

Wonderful! I thought. I wrote back quickly, to ask where
he found the information, and he wrote back that it was in a
book called *Flight Fantastic*, by Annette Carson. "The most
comprehensive history of aerobatics ever written," he said.
I thanked him again and sat back in my chair.

Yet this is when the other details began to wander in and
trouble the easy first take. I could imagine some pilot long
ago turning a slow, graceful horizontal pirouette in the clear
sky over France. But I realized I did not know where the town
of Juvisy was. And I did not know what a Henri Farman biplane was. Back at my computer with Google Earth, I typed
in "Juvisy, France," and nearly gasped out loud when the
planet spun on my screen and the descending view landed
just south of Paris and nearly on one of the main runways
at Orly Airport! I am certain I made some noise when I next
looked for images of a Henri Farman biplane, and what the
computer showed me was a stick and linen and wire con-
traption less sturdy looking than the plane at Kitty Hawk.
He flew a roll in that? Who was this guy?

Hours later now, I know the man was a character. He flew
under bridges, and landed up to his axles in water just to impress his friends who were watching. And I've learned that
Juvisy was the place pilots wondered how far they could push
their machines. Only four years before Chevillard turned his
airplane over and smiled at his friends, a pilot named Eu-
gène Lefebvre flew dives and steep banks over the town of

Reims at the first world air meet and was credited with the planet's first aerobatic performance. Then one month later, he crashed a Wright biplane at Juvisy when his controls jammed and became the first pilot of a powered airplane to lose his life. (Oddly, the death of the first passenger happened one year earlier, in 1908, back in the States, with Orville Wright at the controls.) And I learned that 1913 was a hard and difficult year. The highest temperature ever recorded in the United States was 134°F, set on July 10, 1913. And in November, as Chevillard flew over the southern reaches of Paris, a storm settled over the Great Lakes that even today is called the worst, most devastating storm to cross those waters. A minimum of 235 lives were lost, and more than forty ships went down.

But the image of an open, fragile biplane sticks in my head. In 1913 Adolphe Pégoud was the first man to fly upside down. In 1913, Petr Nikolaevich Nesterov, a lieutenant in the Russian Army, flew the first 360-degree loop. How sturdy and tight those planes must have seemed to pilots back then. How safe and secure in the sky. What coincidence of wonder and confidence occurred in Chevillard's mind as he imagined turning his airplane upside down and then all the way around to level flight again? What gasps came from the people on the ground?

If he could fly a roll in that paper airplane, I think, then surely I will be able to fly one in something larger, faster, stronger, better.

The roads north of Fargo and west of the interstate highway are ice covered and slick. On the phone a few days ago, Barb told me Jake would stop flying when the snow fell, because he wasn't going to plow the strip this year, and yesterday two or three inches fell from the overnight sky, our first real snow of the winter, my heart sinking with every flake because I believed this flight would need to wait until March, or April, or May, when the snow melted and the waterlogged strip would dry and be ready for traffic. But then this morning Jake called and asked when I would be there.

"Oh," he said, "there's hardly any snow. Not enough to bother us."

So I told him I would be there at noon. High noon.

I pull into the driveway and then up close to the garage. When I knock on the front door I hear fast feet hustle to the door and then smile when Barb's face is the one I see. Jake's not home, she says. He'll be right back with the pickup, and I should probably move my Jeep to let him park. So I head back and put the Jeep in reverse, and already Jake is pulling up next to me and then beyond.

"You all ready?" he calls.

"You bet," I reply. "Should I bring my headset?"

"Bring everything you've got," he says.

We do not head straight for the plane. Jake's been working all morning, and it's lunchtime. Barb has made a wonderful potato soup, he says, and offers me a bowl. Ever the engineer, Jake wants to talk physics a bit, the mechanics of the roll. He hands me a few copies of the magazine *Sport Aerobatics*, a textbook called *Basic Aerobatics*, and a copy of the one book that's a classic for pilots: *Stick and Rudder*, by Wolfgang Langewiesche.

"I know this book," I say.

"You've read it?" Jake asks.

"Yep. And his other one, too. I even know his son, William."

Jake nods and we sit at a kitchen table. Suddenly, I feel a need to remind him of a confession I made.

"Jake," I say, "remember that I have never flown a stick, and I have never flown a tail dragger."

"I thought you had some time in a Citabria," he says.

"I was supposed to," I say. "But there was a problem with the airplane. I called the instructor, and he said the line guys pushed it into the hangar. I said that was great, the plane would be nice and warm. And he said no, you don't understand. They pushed it *into* the hangar. They damaged a wingtip."

"Well," Jake says, referring to my lack of experience, "it shouldn't matter that much."

That much, I think. We talk about wing loading and lift, and we talk about the stresses on an airplane during maneuvers and then at stall speeds.

"Think about it," he says. "When you're flying straight and level, you have one G pulling you down, gravity, and one G pulling you up, lift. But when you're inverted, the wings are pulling you down. You have two Gs going down, so you need to have two Gs of forward stick to keep the plane level."

It makes sense, in an abstract way. But I cannot imagine what this will feel like when the airplane is in my hands.

Before too long, however, we're going through the steps to make an airplane roll.

"Here's what I know," I say, wanting to sound like I've done my homework. "From straight and level, you pitch the nose up about twenty degrees, then give it just a bit of forward stick to stop the climb. You give it full deflection of the ailerons one way or the other, and keep it that way until you're all the way around. You stop the roll when the horizon is pretty much level again, and you should be pointed about twenty degrees down. You pull back for straight and level, and you should be done."

"Pretty close," Jake says. "Not everything, but pretty close."

The walk from Jake and Barb's house to the hangar is a short one past farmstead outbuildings and under trees, a firm pathway already established in the new snow. We enter the hangar by a side door, and Jake finds the button to raise the huge folding door for the airplanes. Sunlight fills the space. In the back of the hangar, a large four-wheel-drive Case New Holland farm tractor of some sort waits for summer. In front of it, a Cessna 210 owned by one of Jake's friends. In front of the Cessna is a tiny ultralight with bright-orange wings, owned by some other friend. And in front of the ultralight, red and white with a light-gold stripe down the middle, shooting stars on the tail and wings and wheel pants, the Super Decathlon 8KCAB. High winged and fabric skin, this plane has a 180-horsepower Lycoming engine. Fuel and oil systems for inverted flight. Aileron spades. Two-blade constant-speed propeller. Tandem seats with rear controls. Fully aerobatic rating. Just under thirty feet long with a wingspan of thirty-two feet, this plane can pull six positive Gs, and five negative Gs. It can climb 1,280 feet a minute and fly 155 miles per hour at sea level. This is not an airplane made for going somewhere. This is an airplane made to fly.

Jake adds a bit of fuel and pushes the airplane out of the

hangar. We each put on a parachute, and then Jake tells me I get to fly from the backseat.

"Normally," he says, "a tail-wheel instructor would have you fly from the front. But I've never landed this from the back."

"Good reason to fly up front," I agree.

I climb in, and he helps me secure the four-point harness. As he climbs in I plug in my headset, and soon enough the engine comes to life. Looking up and then past his left shoulder, I have a small concern.

"Jake," I say, "the only instrument I can see is the airspeed indicator. If I get this thing all screwy, you're going to have to let me know."

"Oh, I wouldn't worry about that," he says.

He can't see me because he's looking forward, watching his gauges, but my smile in the backseat is huge. Frankly, I am not worried at all. I thought I would be. I thought there would be some fear, some anxiety, or at the very least that creeping feeling of being somewhat of an impostor, of being into something a bit over my head. But the feeling I have this afternoon is completely different. Every airplane I have ever flown has had side-by-side seating. Every airplane I have ever flown has had a wheel instead of a stick and tricycle landing gear instead of a tail wheel. But as we wait just a moment for the engine temperatures, the cylinder-head and exhaust-gas temperatures, to rise, it occurs to me that there is something else going on. It would almost be wrong to say I am inside this airplane. It would be more accurate to say I am wearing it. The stick is a little lower than I expected it would be, but already I know this is a change for the better.

The roll, of course, is no longer anything special. There is no question anymore about the ability of the airplane. The Super Decathlon is built for just this purpose. So are the Citabria, the biplane Pitts Special, and a hundred other planes whose designers saw them waltzing and jitterbugging and tangoing through the sky before the first drawing was made. And, in truth, it would be difficult to find an airplane that cannot successfully roll. The little Cessna 152 Aerobat model, which can roll with the best of them, is different from the non-Aerobat only in the addition of an inverted fuel and oil system, wing spars from the Cessna 172, and tighter seat belts. And what is perhaps the most famous roll of all time took place in a Boeing prototype, the 367-80, the model that would become both the KC-135 Stratotanker and the Boeing 707 passenger jet. Demonstrating the prototype for the crowd at a hydroplane race on Lake Washington in Seattle on August 7, 1955, test pilot Tex Johnston brought the plane in fast and low over the water, four hundred miles per hour and only four hundred feet above the waves, and proceeded to roll the thing in front of the company president, who had no idea he was going to do that, and a few thousand petrified and then amazed others. Then to prove it wasn't a mistake, he did it again.

The real question this afternoon is not if the airplane can roll, but if I can. Jake gives the plane a bit of throttle, and we begin to taxi. The runway at Jake's is thirty-three hundred feet long. And in a way I can say I've landed here a hundred times. The strip is part of the Microsoft Flight Simulator, and with a computer-generated Cub I've landed here, and everywhere else I've ever wanted to visit. But the computer version has very little to do with real life. Only thirteen hundred feet of the runway have been cleared of snow, and those thirteen hundred feet seem very narrow.

"You can steer us down to the end," Jake tells me.

"I can't see a thing!" I say. Tail draggers sit nose high, and the backseat view on the ground is notoriously bad. This is why you will sometimes see tail draggers weaving S-turns on the ground as they taxi—it's so the pilot can get a glimpse of the distance ahead. I cannot see anything in front of us.

"I'll let you know when we get to the end," he says.

With my feet on the rudder pedals, I manage to keep us out of the deeper snow by looking out the side windows, but when we get to the end Jake takes over and turns us into the wind. The throttle goes forward. The deep rush of engine and prop grows loud. It's time to go flying.

We begin, picking up speed. After a very short distance, I can feel Jake give the plane a bit of forward stick to raise the tail, and very shortly after that we are airborne. There is that unmistakable, and every time thrilling, feeling of the wheels leaving the earth, that friction no longer transmitted through the plane's body to my own, a tangible distance opening between airplane and earth. I love that moment. It shifts everything.

We climb. Barely past the cleared part of the runway, and still over the farmstead, Jake puts us in a sharp 45-degree bank to the west. The motion is sudden, a snap bank if the name could apply, and for a moment I wonder if he is testing my stomach, or my willingness to continue. We pull hard around to the northwest and then level the wings, though we continue to climb.

"This is fun!" I say.

"Why don't you fly us while I use the radio?" Jake says.

I take the stick and press my feet to the rudder pedals. Just to get the feel of the thing, I make a small turn to the left, and then a small turn to the right. So tight! I think. The stick is firm and easy in my hand, much more responsive than I imagined. Like driving a showroom Porsche. Jake calls Air Traffic Control, Fargo Approach, and lets them know we're in the air. I follow a railway toward the town of Prosper. Below us, the snow-covered flatland prairie is punctuated by farmsteads and roadways, a white table with pools and lines of brown. The clouds, grown a bit thicker since this morning, are the same white as the snow, and where they meet in the far distance the horizon is fluid, shifting, and beautiful.

"Jake," I say, "are those towers going to be any bother?" Below us, and just ahead, a group of radio antennae, each one painted red and white to be visible to airplanes, is growing close.

"We're well above those," Jake says. "Anyway, why don't you turn us to the south?"

I turn the Super Decathlon to the south, a slow, easy turn with a bank just beyond 45 degrees, until we're heading into the wind.

"Let me run you through it once," he says, "just to get the feel of it. Okay?"

"Let's do it," I say happily.

Jake puts the plane into a shallow dive, and I watch the airspeed indicator climb. When we reach 140 miles per hour, Jake pulls back on the stick and puts the nose about 30 degrees above the horizon. Then there's a bit of forward stick to stop the climb, and we are weightless, at the top of an arc, honestly floating four thousand feet above the North Dakota prairie.

"Roll!" Jake says, and the stick goes hard left.

The plane rolls. From the outside, what you would see is a stationary world and a colorful airplane whose left wing drops. The plane goes on what is called knife-edge, wings straight up and down, but does not stop there. The plane continues to turn and is quickly upside down, then on knife-edge again the other way, and then right side up. But from the inside, it's not so much the plane that moves as the world around it. When Jake pushes the stick hard left I watch the left side of the horizon rise. The planet turns around a point defined by the nose of the airplane. The horizon is sideways, and then completely backward with farms in the "up" and the heavens in the "down," and then sideways the other way. Finally the stick comes back to center, and the horizon is where it should be. We are pointed just a little bit down. One G all the way around. I never felt even the smallest tug away from my seat.

"How did that feel?" Jake asks me.

"That was wonderful!" I exclaim.

"Your turn," he says.

Stick in my hand, I push the nose of the airplane down. I watch the airspeed indicator over Jake's shoulder, and when it hits 140 I pull back. At about 30 degrees above the horizon—I cannot see the attitude indicator, the artificial horizon, so this is at best a guess—I push forward on the stick. Perhaps a little too much because I am suddenly weightless in my seat, and I can feel Barb's potato soup rise in my stomach. But I push the stick left and the world turns.

I remember my first drum lesson. In some upstairs studio at a music store, the teacher sat me down at a drum set, a real one and not a set of quiet pads, and taught me a simple jazz riff on the cymbals, snare, and bass drum. No sheet music. Just here, here's how you do it, give it a shot. When I had the feel of the thing he walked over to a set of vibraphones and pulled out red mallets. In time with my beat, he began a blues tune. I do not remember which one. It was simple, evocative, and I was transported someplace a long way away from that small room. We played for the scheduled half hour. He'd teach me some small variation to the riff, and then we'd get back to it. I'd invent some stretch of my own, and, awkward as it was, he found a way to follow me and keep the song going. I don't think either of us ever stopped smiling.

When the lesson was over, he did give me music. Rudiments to study and practice and learn, but when the week was over and we met again, we used that learning to make the half-hour jam a bit deeper, a bit faster, a bit more on edge. I do not remember this guy's name, or why I stopped taking lessons from him—I think he found a better job—but I do know that every drum teacher after him sat me down at pads and we went over the drills, the eight or sixteen or twenty-four lines of music from some textbook I was supposed to practice for that week. Not one of them ever played a song. I joined school orchestras and ensembles, of course, and with friends made very bad high school rock-and-roll bands, but none of it ever held the magic of those first few lessons until a good many years later, at a blues bar called the Hot L Warren, just north of Amherst, Massachusetts, where a friend was playing piano in a small group and their drummer let me sit in. Doug smiled at me over his shoulder, and we were off. I followed him and he followed me. The bass player joined us both, and I'm not sure any one of us knew where we were going, but oh it was fun.

In other words, you learn how to do something, and when you get good enough, the technique moves from your head to your heart. Knowing the rules and the forms got you here, but now that you're here, you stop thinking about the rules because here is fresh territory. It is the same feeling, the same desire, that took you to the very first lesson.

The airplane moves past knife-edge to inverted, to knife-edge again, and then almost level. I straighten the stick too early, not expecting the response of the ailerons and wings to be so fast, and end the roll before it is done. A simple correction to the left is all it takes to be level, and then a bit of back pressure on the stick, but it is an ugly finish to a graceful turn.

"I stopped too early," I say.

"Everyone does that," Jake says. "Want to try again?"

I push the plane into the dive, then pull back, then push forward, then hard left again and watch the prairie turn upside down and over itself. This roll I wait for, and end a bit cleaner. But as much as I want to get it right, I am really not very interested in the kind of precision that makes a good aerobatics pilot win competitions and awards. There is beauty in this maneuver, and you can feel it inside the plane.

We've flown a bit too far south to stay in the practice area, so I turn us to the north, and we fly level for a bit. Jake teaches me how to fly a basic wingover, which is just a small climb and then a hard bank, the plane falling a bit as it changes direction, another move that from the ground seems more poetry than aerodynamics, and when we're back in the right place for Air Traffic Control I get to try another roll.

This roll does not go so well. I dive, and then pull up, but when I go to push forward and then hard left, Jake's voice is fast in my headset.

"You've got your nose way too high on this one," he says, and I can feel his hand on the front stick, correcting my mistake.

"Sorry about that," I say.

"Oh, it's nothing," Jake says. "The faster you're going, the faster you roll. If you're not going very fast, then the roll is very slow and more difficult to control. You were climbing so much we were getting near stall speed. That just wouldn't be very much fun for a first time out."

Still feeling the soup a bit higher in my chest than I'd like, I couldn't agree more. But we get the plane back on an even trim, and it's my turn to try again.

"Why do we have to dive when we do this?" I ask.

"Just airspeed," he says. "It saves time. We could push the power forward and wait for the plane to speed up, but this is faster and saves gas."

This time the steps come together. I'm not thinking, Do this, then this, then this. Not really so worried about getting my feet exactly on the painted shoe prints on the studio floor. Or, to be more honest, I am thinking, Do this, then this, but not so much as to get it right as to have fun, to fly an airplane past upside down in the sky, to make something beautiful. I still pull out of the roll too early, but I know I can learn this patience as I learn this airplane.

"Jake," I say, "you have no idea how good this feels back here."

We head back to the farmstead. I fly the plane until we're on final approach, but I cannot see the landing strip from the backseat, and do not know how to land a tail dragger anyway, so Jake takes over and lands us gently in the new snow. We taxi, then push the plane into the hangar.

Half an hour later, I am back in my own home, a cup of coffee in my hand, a collie begging for a walk. So we go outside to play in the yard, and I watch the commercial jets as well as the little props arc through the air. I already know I'm hooked. I do not have the wish to compete, but some afternoon, and with luck many afternoons in the future, heading out or coming in from some other flight, I will say a prayer of thanks for Maurice Chevillard, Tex Johnston, and Jake Gust. I'll put whatever I am flying into a brief dive, then pull back, then push forward, and then hard left or right, and I will watch the world dance around me. With luck, on the ground, someone will have heard the changing pitch of the sound and looked up. And with luck, they will smile.

Bad Form

There are ways to do things badly—

NTSB Identification: CHI07CA087.
The docket is stored in the Docket Management System
(DMS). Please contact Records Management Division
14 CFR Part 91: General Aviation
Accident occurred Friday, March 09, 2007 in La Crosse WI
Probable Cause Approval Date: 6/27/2007
Aircraft: Cessna 150, registration: N72725
Injuries: 2 Uninjured.

The airplane was substantially damaged when it struck a
snowbank during final approach to landing. The certified
flight instructor stated that the accident landing approach
was normal until the airplane was on about 1/2 mile final
where the student pilot extended the flaps to 40 degrees.
The instructor stated that he then "fell asleep for 20 to 25
seconds." He stated that he opened his eyes just prior to the
wheels hitting the snowbank. He stated that he did not have

enough time to react to prevent the impact. The airplane's nose landing gear collapsed and the airplane slid to a stop. The flight instructor stated that his inability to remain awake was due to a lack of sleep the night before.

The National Transportation Safety Board determines the probable cause(s) of this accident as follows:

The dual student's failure to maintain the proper glidepath and clearance from terrain and the flight instructor's delayed remedial action. A factor was the flight instructor's fatigue.

And there are those times when what happens seems to have never happened before—

NTSB Identification: SEA07CA103.
The docket is stored in the Docket Management System
(DMS). Please contact Records Management Division
14 CFR Part 91: General Aviation
Accident occurred Tuesday, April 17, 2007 in Oak Glen CA
Probable Cause Approval Date: 6/27/2007
Aircraft: Cessna 152, registration: N49902
Injuries: 2 Minor.

The flight instructor said that he had the student under the hood and was giving him headings to follow. He said that as they approached the mountains the aircraft began to lose altitude. The flight instructor said that he took control of the airplane and attempted to maneuver the airplane out of the downdraft. He said that even with full power, the aircraft settled and impacted a tree. He said the airplane "spun around 180 degrees and landed in a small stream [approximately 2 inches deep] on its landing gear." The flight instructor said that the airplane was destroyed.

The National Transportation Safety Board determines the probable cause(s) of this accident as follows: The flight instructor's failure to maintain clearance from trees while maneuvering. Contributing factors were the downdraft weather condition, and the tree.

There are ways to be stupid—

NTSB Identification: CHI07CA111.
The docket is stored in the Docket Management System (DMS). Please contact Records Management Division
14 CFR Part 91: General Aviation
Accident occurred Sunday, April 22, 2007 in Paw Paw MI
Probable Cause Approval Date: 6/27/2007
Aircraft: Cessna 150F, registration: N8893S
Injuries: 1 Minor.

The airplane impacted trees and terrain while on final approach. The pilot stated that he was landing on a private grass airstrip toward the north. The pilot described the weather as a "clear day, but with high winds." The pilot reported that while on final approach he encountered "wind shear straight down." The pilot stated that the airplane "clipped the tree tops" before impacting terrain. The pilot reported the airplane came to rest along a tree line near the west edge of the north–south runway. The pilot stated that the accident could have been prevented if he had not attempted flight in the high/gusting wind conditions or by entering final approach at a higher altitude. The wind conditions at an airport approximately 15 nautical miles from the accident site were reported to be from 200 magnetic degrees at 9 knots, gusting to 16 knots. The pilot's medical and student pilot certificate had expired 20 months prior to the accident. The pilot's most recent 90-day solo endorsement was dated September 17, 2003.

The National Transportation Safety Board determines the probable cause(s) of this accident as follows:

The student pilot's inadequate compensation for wind conditions while on final approach. Contributing factors to the accident were the gusting wind conditions and the trees.

And there are ways to be caught off guard—

NTSB Identification: DFW07CA099.
The docket is stored in the Docket Management System
(DMS). Please contact Records Management Division
14 CFR Part 91: General Aviation
Accident occurred Friday, April 27, 2007 in San Antonio TX
Probable Cause Approval Date: 6/27/2007
Aircraft: Cessna 152, registration: N49108
Injuries: 2 Uninjured.

The single-engine airplane was blown over by the jet blast of a departing twin-turbine powered airliner while taxiing. The single-engine airplane had been instructed by the ATC ground controller to taxi to a parking area via a taxiway that crossed behind the waiting airliner. Meanwhile, the scheduled airliner was issued a takeoff clearance. As the airliner powered-up to enter the active runway for departure, the jet blast rolled the single-engine airplane over to an inverted position. The private pilot and passenger were able to exit the airplane unassisted. The single-engine airplane's right wing sustained structural damage. The airliner, unaware of what had occurred, departed the airport. According to the Aeronautical

Information Manual, chapter 7, paragraph 7-3-8 a, ". . . the flight disciplines necessary to ensure vortex avoidance during VFR operations must be exercised by the pilot." According to FAA order 7110.65R, ground controllers are to "Use caution when taxiing smaller aircraft/helicopters in the vicinity of larger aircraft."

The National Transportation Safety Board determines the probable cause(s) of this accident as follows:

The single-engine pilot's failure to avoid the jet blast while taxiing and the ground controller's inattentiveness to the situation, which resulted in the airplane's being blown over.

Yet here is a truth. If there is a problem, an emergency in the air, chances are someone else has had that problem before. Someone else has figured out what to do, and all I have to do is follow his lead. If there is an electrical fire during flight, there is a checklist, a procedure for putting out the fire, for getting down safely. Master switch off. Other switches off. Ignition switch on. Vents closed. Cabin heat and air closed. Activate extinguisher. After the fire is out, master switch on. Check circuit breakers. Vents open. Cabin heat and air open. Land as soon as practical.

Likewise, if there is an engine fire, the steps are already written down. If the radios fail, if I get lost, if I suspect problems with carbon monoxide or hypoxia, the paths are clear. Every pilot learns these steps and commits them to memory.

But knowing what to do and remembering what to do when the world gets fast can be very different things. More than once during my flight training, the instructor leaned over and pulled the engine throttle all the way back. "You've just had an engine failure," he said. "What are you going to do?"

The routine is simple. Pitch for best glide speed. Go through the checklist for restarting the engine. If that doesn't work, pick a good place to land. There's plenty of time. Unless the airplane is flying very low, there are miles and miles of distance before the wheels touch the ground. Once my instructor pulled the throttle back when we were on the downwind leg for a landing, just a thousand feet above the ground. Best glide speed and two turns to the left put us perfect form for what is called a cowboy landing, a swooping, descending curve to the runway, then an easy level off, flare, and landing. When we had come to a stop, I told him the drill was good practice. Then I told him it was fun.

So why do airplanes fall out of the sky? According to the Department of Transportation's Bureau of Transportation Statistics Web site, in 2003 632 people died in general aviation accidents. For a bit of context, though, in that same year, 42,643 people died in highway accidents; 951 died in railway accidents, 886 in boating accidents. There were 1,741 general aviation accidents. There were 6,328,000 traffic accidents. There are Web sites devoted to airplane crashes, maudlin displays of wreckage and pain. There are audio files of pilots who believe, rightly or wrongly, they are about to die. There are psychologists who specialize in treating the fear of flying. What bothers passengers, of course, isn't really the risk or the danger. Every other way of getting about is more likely to cause them harm. With flying, it is the feeling of helplessness, of vulnerability. If things go screwy, there's nothing they can do.

For pilots, however, it all comes down to just two things. Just two ways for the grace of an airplane to turn ugly and tragic. First, the machine can break. It can break in a thousand ways, some of them known, a few of them fresh. But there are rules for inspections, time periods that cannot be exceeded, and an army of mechanics and officials working to make sure the parts stay together. Second, the pilot can fly in bad form. He can fly beyond his talent or experience or capability, or he can fly the plane beyond its design. Every moment of every flight depends on the decision making of the pilot in command. There is rarely a second chance.

Every airplane lands. Some more gracefully than others, some as awkwardly as a teenager on a first date, some so smoothly it would compare to the kiss of an angel.
    Then again, there is always room for the simply bizarre—

NTSB Identification: DCA07WA053
Scheduled 14 CFR Non-U.S., Commercial
operation of Ryanair
Accident occurred Monday, June 25, 2007 in
Treviso, Italy
Aircraft: Boeing B737-800, registration: EI-CSN
Injuries: 181 Uninjured.

At 15:46 European Summer Time, the crew of a Boeing 737-800, Irish registration EI-CSN, operating as Ryan Air flight 9513, from Gerona, Spain to Treviso, Italy, found the left nose wheel missing after landing. During landing, the crew reported a "loud bang" and discovered the wheel was missing and the nose gear axle fractured during post-flight inspection. The left nose wheel has not been located.

And sadly, there is also room for those who should know better—

NTSB Identification: ATL07FA077

14 CFR Part 91: General Aviation

Accident occurred Sunday, April 22, 2007 in Hamilton GA

Aircraft: Beech 58, registration: N5647C

Injuries: 5 Fatal.

This is preliminary information, subject to change, and may contain errors. Any errors in this report will be corrected when the final report has been completed.

On April 22, 2007, about 1451 eastern daylight time, a Beech BE-58, N5647C, registered to Renaissance Aircraft Management LLC, operating as a 14 CFR Part 91 personal flight, broke up in flight in the vicinity of Hamilton, Georgia. Visual meteorological conditions prevailed and no flight plan was filed. The airplane was destroyed. The private pilot and 4 passengers were fatally injured. The flight originated from Jack Edwards Airport, Gulf Shores, Alabama, at about 1300 central daylight time.

A witness stated he was in his boat fishing in a lake in the vicinity of his home. He heard an airplane approaching his location from the southeast to the northwest. It sounded as if the pilot was performing some acrobatic maneuvers. The witness looked up and could not see the airplane. The engine noise continued to increase in intensity and the witness observed the airplane to the north of the lake heading northwest. The airplane was high and descending very fast in a 45 to 60 degree nose down attitude. The witness stated he observed a wing or part of the tail separate from the airplane in the vicinity of Hamilton Mulberry Grove Road. He immediately went to his boat dock and to his home and called the 911 emergency operators to report the accident.

A motorist approached a Georgia State Patrol Officer at the accident scene and informed the officer that he was a friend of the deceased pilot. He further informed the officer that he was planning on purchasing an airplane from the pilot, and the pilot was going to use the money from the sale of the airplane to purchase the Beech 58 that he was flying at the time of the accident. The motorist further stated that the accident pilot's "flying skills were below his standards because the pilot was known for overstressing the planes he flew." The motorist further stated from having flown with him and he made a statement to a friend about three weeks ago that the accident pilot would probably crash an airplane within the next year.

A friend of the pilot stated the pilot was in his shop on Friday, April 20, 2007, before he departed to Gulf Shores, Alabama on a fishing trip in his Beech 58. The friend informed the pilot, "That he thought he was stupid and not to do anything in the airplane that would get him hurt." The pilot stated, "I think I can roll this airplane." The friend stated, "The pilot had been at Sun N' Fun in Lakeland, Florida, during the week and had observed a performer rolling a Beech 18, and the deceased pilot just kept the rolling issue in his head." The friend stated the pilot had flown with a retired airline pilot, who owns a Beech 55, and the pilot had rolled the airplane with the deceased pilot as a passenger.

Another friend of the deceased pilot stated, he was in the right front seat of the airplane on April 19, 2007, on a return flight from Sun N' Fun in Lakeland, Florida, with two other passengers in the back seats. They departed Lakeland, Florida, and the pilot climbed to an initial cruising altitude of 9,500 feet. The autopilot was on and the airplane was cruising at 220 knots. The pilot climbed to 10,500 feet to see if they could get a better ground speed and eventually descended back down to 9,500 feet. A short time later, the pilot stated, "I want to try something." The pilot rolled the airplane to the left side, and then back to the right side with the autopilot off and stated, "I believe it's possible to roll this airplane."

The pilot pushed down on the control yoke, initiated a descent, and turned the airplane to the left, pulled back on the control yoke, and the airplane went up and over to the right like a spiral until the airplane was in a knife-edge attitude. The friend of the pilot stated he did not know what airspeed they obtained while the pilot was performing this maneuver and stated, "It got me out of my comfort zone, and I could not handle it." The friend stated he grabbed the flight controls, leveled the airplane, and stated to the pilot, "I cannot do this." The pilot replied, "I believe it is possible to roll this airplane." The pilot descended down to 7,500 feet and leveled off in cruise flight, and there was no further discussion about rolling the airplane. A short time later, the pilot pulled the power back on the right engine, feathered the propeller, and they continued towards Griffin, Georgia, in cruise flight. The pilot started the engine, and they made their descent and landing at Griffin.

Dreams of Flying

1.

There is a flying saucer in my backyard.

Gunmetal gray, it hovers for a minute near the ash and maple trees in the winter twilight, then turns sharply toward the ditch and flies at amazing speed barely inches off the ground. I am convinced it is going to thrust a hole into my neighbor's house, but then it veers again and heads toward the pond. There is no engine noise. No lights. No sound at all, except the rush of the wind. Its maneuvers would render any human pilot senseless.

Then the wind dies, and the saucer flops into a snowbank. A small child in a thick coat and snow pants runs after her errant toy and drags it back to her friends and their sleds. Once again at the top of the slope that leads down into the shallow ditch, she climbs into the saucer and rides the thing, screaming in delight, until she disappears.

But there is something in the way it made that turn, I think. Something in the way it graced around the trees. Something in the way it gathered the wind.

2.

KFAR 022320Z 030024 35025G35KT 1SM-SN BLSN BKN008

3.

After a century of flying, we still live at a moment of emergence like that experienced by creatures first escaping from the sea. For us the emergence has been given meaning because we can think about it, and can perhaps understand the nature of our liberation. Mechanical wings allow us to fly, but it is with our minds that we make the sky ours. The old measures of distance no longer apply, in part because we hop across the globe in single sittings, but also because in doing so we visit a place which even just above our homes is as exotic and revealing as the most foreign destination.

—WILLIAM LANGEWIESCHE, *Inside the Sky*

4.

KFAR TEMPO 0408 VRB30G40KT 2SM TSRAGR OVC025CB

5.

I know a man, a pilot, a reporter who is most often overseas in some dismal or violent place, who once wrote me an e-mail when I asked what he read for pleasure. "Mostly technical sailing drivel," he replied. And when those words lit my computer screen, I will admit I sat back in my chair and smiled.

So many connections, I thought. When I was twelve or thirteen and spending part of my summer days at a day camp north of Chicago, one of our activities was to take canoes and very small sailboats out on an exaggerated pond surrounded by elm and oak and maple trees and try to get the hang of things. The canoes were easy. Even if I never learned a single textbook stroke, I could make them go where I wanted with ease. But the sailboats were special. I had no language for it back then, and barely any now, but when we pushed away from the bank and tightened a line, the moment when the wind filled the sail and I could feel that power rush down the mast and through the lines to the hull, and then watch the boat move forward, that moment was soul filling and huge. A hand on the tiller then, an eye on the sail, and suddenly I was using nothing less than the whole force of the planet to make the boat head out.

When we were in the canoes, we had a destination. The pond had an island with a fire ring, and there was a small strait that led to another part of the pond, mostly hidden by what I remember as extravagant willow trees. We would paddle to the island, or to the other pond, beach our canoes, and find some way to nearly get in trouble. But when we were sailing, destination was nowhere in our minds. The act itself, the motion, the sense of sensing wind and how tightly to pull in some line (we did not know enough to call them sheets) was everything.

Fast-forward several years to a summer on a lake in central Missouri, and I am working at a hotel marina, gassing powerboats that pull to the dock, renting powerboats to hotel guests. Tethered to buoys in the hotel cove are three sailboats. One of them is a twenty-four-foot-long Bristol sloop with an enclosed cabin. Old and dirty, without any technical or aesthetic frills, it sat in the cove ostensibly for rent, ignored by everyone except those driving powerboats around it.

"You know," I said to the dock manager one day, "I can sail that thing."

He looked at me, wondering what I was up to. Sailing was nowhere in his experience. This was a lake for water-skiing and high-speed cruising. I doubt he'd ever been on a boat under sail.

"Go ahead," he said to me. The day had been slow. "Air it out."

I swam out to the boat and hauled myself up over the side and into the cockpit. Then down into the cabin where I discovered two sails, a main and a jib, stuffed into the forward bunk. I knew enough to get them connected to the mast. Then I unhooked from the buoy, raised the mainsail, and began to pray. Pray for wind. Pray for the knowledge of what to do next to come back from memory or leap forward from the obvious. The sail filled, the sheets tightened, and the boat began to turn into the wind. But one hand on the tiller and the other on the line, I could *feel* the angle that would move us out of the cove and into the open areas of the lake. This was a small boat, easily handled by one person, so I raised the jib and passed the dock at a fair clip, heeled over enough to look exciting, happy at my good fortune. I had no place to go. The wind on the lake was strong. I was simply heading out.

What I did not know then was how close this was to flying. For the sailor, tacking into the wind is, for all that really matters, the same thing as crabbing into the wind for pilots. Part of it is technique. A lot of it is feel. Pilots and sailors know what the weather is, what it is forecast to become, and what it might become instead. Wind speed and wind direction mean everything. There are parts of the language that show the connections. Sailors work from a cockpit. People speak of flying a spinnaker. And there is a type of glider called a sailplane. Bad weather can sink a ship as fast as it can down an airplane. I would not be surprised if every pilot had some sailing experience. I would not be surprised if every sailor had a dream of becoming a pilot.

Much later that afternoon, after several comic attempts to get reconnected to the buoy as it slid alongside the hull, one of the other dockworkers came out to collect me in a small powerboat.

"We were watching you," he said. "You were really flying."

6.

KFAR 101053Z AUTO 31035G50KT 10SM SCT021 BKN 033 16/12 A2962 RMK AO2 PK WND 29053/1035 SLP027 T01560117 TSNO

7.

Returning astronauts almost always fall into a deep depression. They are stricken with an uncontrollable desire to gain weight. At dusk you will see them circling the park in silk pajamas, mocked by children, trailed by dogs. Prolonged weightlessness destroys the bones, the muscles, and, eventually, the larynx, which is why when astronauts return to earth we find that their speech has been reduced to a kind of quiet piping, at once soft and shrill, that is intelligible only to other astronauts, a piping that approaches, but is not, despite the government's assertion, song.

—BEN LERNER, *Angle of Yaw*

8.

In flight, the stick no longer felt disconnected and dead. It stood up, and there was life in it. When you moved it, it nudged back against your hand. I moved it more, and came against an elastic resistance. There was a will in it, soft, elastic, but unmistakably a will.

—WOLFGANG LANGEWIESCHE, *America from the Air*

9.

Thus is the earth at once a desert and a paradise, rich in secret hidden gardens, gardens inaccessible, but to which the craft leads us ever back, one day or another. Life may scatter us and keep us apart; it may prevent us from thinking very often of one another; but we know that our comrades are somewhere "out there"—where, one can hardly say—silent, forgotten, but deeply faithful. And when our path crosses theirs, they greet us with such manifest joy, shake us so gaily by the shoulders! Indeed we are accustomed to waiting.

—ANTOINE DE SAINT-EXUPERY, *Wind, Sand, and Stars*

10.

And yet there's something even deeper, something even more seductive, about exploring one of the millions of slivers of terra incognita left all across the planet: If no one has been where you're going, you have no idea whether what you want to do *can* be done. The reason to go is to find out. The reason to go is to find out whether *you* can do it. Whether you have the nerve and the craft, the resilience and resourcefulness to think on your feet and dance on your fears.

—MARK JENKINS, *A Man's Life*

11.

An image of ultimacy in an age of polarized light. Will you marry me, skywrites the uncle. A pill to induce awe with a side effect of labor. A lateral inward tilting and the aircraft pushes its envelope. A minor innovation in steering outdates a branch of literature. Envelopes push back. The way a wake turns to ice, then vapor, then paper, uniting our analogues in error, intimacy's highest form. Jet engines are designed to sublimate stray birds. *No* appears in the corn.

—BEN LERNER, *Angle of Yaw*

12.

KFAR 030253Z AUTO 35028G34KT 10SM CLR 05/M11 A2982 RMK AO2 PK WND 35035/0235 SLP107 T00501106 53027 TSNO

13.

And thus, also, the realities of nature resume their pride of place. It is not with metal that the pilot is in contact. Contrary to the vulgar illusion, it is thanks to the metal, and by virtue of it, that the pilot rediscovers nature. As I have already said, the machine does not isolate man from the great problems of nature but plunges him more deeply into them.

—ANTOINE DE SAINT-EXUPERY, *Wind, Sand, and Stars*

14.

When I was in eighth grade, my class took a wintertime trip to Washington DC. I have no idea why *any* eighth-grade class would want to do that. We left our suburb, drove down to Chicago, flew to Washington, looked at monuments, and spent the nights dialing other hotel rooms to see who was up and if we could get around the hall monitors and chaperones. I am sure we were supposed to be learning something about government or civics or history, but none of that landed in fertile soil. And frankly, I remember very little of the phone calls or the unsuccessful attempts toward hallway freedom and then the coveted stairwell. I was in eighth grade. The present moment was everything.

Still, I do remember the flight home. Or, to be more exact, what I remember is what I did not know about that flight until after we landed. We were in the air for a very long time, it seemed. We were served extra soda, extra peanuts. At one point, the captain walked down the aisle to a bathroom at the back of the plane. Several flight attendants went with him. And then the word spread through the cabin that the captain had pulled up the bathroom floor and was peering with a flashlight into the belly of the aircraft. Whisper led to whisper. Landing gear. Not going down. Cannot land.

I remember that I had a window seat and I could see the snow falling. I did not know that our parents, all of them, had been told, slowly, about our situation. In the cockpit, the three green lights that say the gear is down and locked did not come on. I did not know that other aircraft were trying to look at us, to see our wheels and relay the news. I did not know that when the decision was made to land, the decision included the full emergency scenario—fire trucks, ambulances, police.

The plane was a TWA flight, and in those days it would have been a 727 or a 707. But the type really did not matter. No plane lands gracefully without wheels or floats or skis. And metal on concrete produces sparks, sparks that could dance into new openings in the wing where the fuel is kept. Spark would become fire. Fire would become explosion. Explosion would remove us all from the grade-school roster.

I remember the approach to the runway, the snow flashing

DREAMS OF FLYING

by in the landing lights, the city lights of Chicago in the distance, the runway and taxiway lights at the airport. And when the airplane touched down—nothing. No collapse. No screeching. No bending of metal. No spark at all. The landing gear held. We pulled up to a gate and got out just like everyone else. Except now we had a story. A story about how we could have died. An airplane story that almost ended badly. Almost. And so we keep it alive, telling and retelling the almost. Because almost is like standing on a ridge, looking into a valley that makes you afraid.

15.

No man can draw a free breath who does not share with other men a common and disinterested ideal. Life has taught us that love does not consist in gazing at each other but in looking outward together in the same direction. There is no comradeship except through unison in the same high effort. Even in our age of material well-being this must be so, else how should we explain the happiness we feel in sharing our last crust with others in the desert? No sociologist's textbook can prevail against this fact. Every pilot who has flown to the rescue of a comrade in distress knows that all joys are vain in comparison with this one.

—ANTOINE DE SAINT-EXUPERY, *Wind, Sand, and Stars*

16.

The one fellow who is really broke in the air is the one who is out of both altitude and speed. *Low and slow* is the pilot's idea of dangerous flying. *Low and fast* is fairly safe if you don't get to daydreaming and hit a tree, and if you don't let them catch you at it, for it is illegal. *High and slow* is fairly

safe if you do it right and if you have trained yourself to react to a stall in such a manner that a prompt recovery will
result instead of a spin. *High and fast*, which your girlfriend
thinks must be awfully dangerous, is the safest. Thus, if you
want to keep well, you have to keep speed or altitude, or
best of all, some of each.

—WOLFGANG LANGEWIESCHE, *Stick and Rudder*

17.

What makes a good paper airplane?

I remember making one that was a thin tube once, with
a loop of paper at each end, the nose loop smaller than the
tail loop. We made it in some science class; it flew pretty
well. And I remember making one that was short, stubby,
and wide, with a heavy nose. It didn't fly so well. There are
books that illustrate and give instructions for a hundred different designs. But the one I make most often is the one we
all make. Fold the paper in half. Fold in the two top quarters
to make a nose. Fold out from there to make a wing. Fold
out again to make it sleek, more supersonic looking. Give
it a gentle push into the middle of the room, maybe aim for
something not so far away.

If the paper is firm and your folds are straight and your
arm is true, the airplane will glide across the room. It will
be nearly perfect. Straight and nearly level. What makes it
exciting, of course, is the fact that we know the universe
conspires to upset the balance. We've made a thousand airplanes that have turned and crashed at our feet, or gone nose
up, stalled, then spun into embarrassment. So many ways
for things to fall out of the sky, even if the sky is just a living room or office. But when it works and the airplane does

what our hearts hope it will (the world record is 27.6 seconds), we smile. Not because we are extraordinary engineers or builders. We are, instead, in some small part, riding that piece of paper across the room, entropy be damned.

18.

Adventure, then, is no longer simply about exploitation or adulation; it's about the quest for understanding. You don't need a mountain or a river or a jungle—you need only an open mind. Your goal does not have to be a first; it need only be something that takes you to a new place and challenges you physically or mentally, emotionally or spiritually.

—MARK JENKINS, *A Man's Life*

19.

Hi Scott,

The phrase that you're looking for is "aer incognitus." Have a nice day.

> Eddie Schmoll
> Professor of Classical Studies
> Concordia College, Moorhead, Minnesota

20.

Striving for superlatives is part of human nature—the highest, the longest, the deepest. But now that many of these goals have been reached, the future of adventure lies in the more subtle, more discriminating endeavors: the most beautiful, the most technical, the project accomplished with the most style. Adventure will be less about simply surviving and more about performing with grace and virtuosity. More personal, more internal, just you and your dream.

Adventure has always been about discovery, but because we and our world are constantly evolving, what we discover is, and forever will be, something new. The golden age of adventure is upon us. Now go.

—MARK JENKINS, *A Man's Life*

21.

KFAR 061607Z 03019KT 1/4SM +SN FZFG OVC005 M01/M02 A2982 RMK AO2 PK WND 04027/1554 P0000

22.

After this era of great pilots is gone, as the era of great sea captains has gone—each nudged aside by the march of inventive genius, by steel cogs and copper discs and hair-thin wires on white faces that are dumb, but speak—it will be found, I think, that all the science of flying has been captured in the breadth of the instrument board, but not the religion of it.

—BERYL MARKHAM, *West with the Night*

23.

Sometimes in August, when the Perseids light the midnight with falling stars, I find myself in a chair in the backyard, marveling at the sky. It doesn't matter that I've seen them before. Every streak of white against the cobalt of space is a thrill and a rush and gasp. I can imagine riding that little piece of rock and ice. I can imagine the poetry of such an intense brief light.

But also in August, when I am waiting for the meteors, I will see a small dot of white moving across the arc of the sky. It seems to go so slowly, though I know very well that it's racing. A satellite in space, catching the sunlight. I do not know which satellite, or which country owns it, or whether its purpose is benign or threatening. All I know is that I can see it, and wonder. For whatever reason, whatever limit there is to my own imagination, I must admit that I do not find the idea of flying in space to be very interesting. Don't misunderstand—I am in favor of every form of spaceflight, a thousand more forms than we have ever tried—but once free of the atmosphere, the flying is all geometry and thrust and gravity and mass. You pilot by mathematics. You cannot stall in outer space. You cannot bank into a turn and watch waves on a lake or deer in a pasture. When we have reached some other planet with an atmosphere, some fluid to move over a wing and give the machine lift, I am sure we will reinvent flying on that planet, with wings and engines to dance in whatever sky there is. It's unlikely I will see it. But I look at that satellite in the August sky, and all I can imagine is the coldness and the quiet.

24.

When you can see the branches of trees from a cockpit, and the shape of rocks no bigger than your own hands, and places where grass thins against sand and becomes yellow, and watch the blow of wind on leaves, you are too close. You are so close that thought is a slow process, useless to you now— even if you can think.

—BERYL MARKHAM, *West with the Night*

25.

KFAR 300053Z 15021G34KT 10SM BKN060 OVC080 05/M01 A2975 RMK AO2 PK WND 15038/0000 SLP086 T00501011

26.

I have imagined teaching the aerial view. The best approach would be apprentice young children as I was apprenticed, to teach them without elaboration simply by flying them to different places, encouraging them to navigate, and to make the translations between maps and the world. Effortlessly they would develop the habit of seeing the world from above, and the more subtle trick while on the ground of understanding scale and orientation of their surroundings. Flying at its best is a way of thinking. Because of that, once having left the earth's surface, people never again quite return to it. But also because of that, adults often find it hard to make the leap. They simply have spent too many years on the ground. To teach them the aerial view you would have to overcome that landlubbing prejudice which equates driving on a country road, or sleeping in a hotel and visiting a restaurant part of town, with having "been" somewhere, to the exclusion of other possibilities.

—WILLIAM LANGEWIESCHE, *Inside the Sky*

27.

A map in the hands of a pilot is a testimony of a man's faith in other men; it is a symbol of confidence and trust. It is not like a printed page that bears mere words, ambiguous and artful, and whose most believing reader—even whose author, perhaps—must allow in his mind a recess for doubt.

A map says to you, "Read me carefully, follow me closely, doubt me not." It says, "I am the earth in the palms of your hand. Without me, you are alone and lost."

—BERYL MARKHAM, *West with the Night*

28.

I still enjoy the escape of low flight and sometimes go out into the desert to chase at head height along dirt roads, banking vertically to make the turns, pulling up to keep the wingtips from dragging. But it is the richness of the genuine aerial view, something both higher and slower, that I keep returning to. I realize now that the aerial view has formed me, and that I have carried it with me from the cockpit to my more recent work of wandering and writing and reporting about the world. And it is odd how even on the ground, weeks from any airplane, the aerial view seems still to fit. It carries with it the possibility of genuinely free movement, and allows just the right amount of participation with the landscape— neither as distant as an old-fashioned vista nor as entrapping as a permanent involvement.

—WILLIAM LANGEWIESCHE, *Inside the Sky*

29.

The storm was a good old-fashioned summer boomer that shook windows and blew small limbs out of trees and gave worried frowns to farmers and car dealers. Rain so hard you couldn't breathe for fear of drowning. Drumbeats hitting the ground. Rifle shots hitting rooftops and windows. Wind so hard you walked at a forward-leaning angle, leaning so hard you knew you'd put your face in the sidewalk if the air were to stop.

The same summer I learned to sail the Bristol sloop, working at a marina in the middle of Missouri, my job was to rent boats to hotel guests, put gas in those boats when they returned, and gas the boats of others who came to the dock.

I was in my first or second year of college and spending my summer in a bathing suit and T-shirt.

When a storm came over the lake, we had what seemed like an emergency drill. Many of the people who rented boats did not know how to drive them very well, and they certainly could not get them into a dock very quickly. So they would approach the dock, we would jump in and power around the slips, whipping the back end around and gunning the reverse to get the boat put away before the next one needed help. It was fast and dramatic and fun work. Storm-drenched tourists stumbling happily up the hill to the resort with a story to tell. Sturm und Drang without the angst.

And when the boats were put away, before the cell passed and the sun came out and once again we untied the boats and reissued the water skis, we were free to watch the weather.

On the day I remember, the wind did not die quickly. Standing on the dock, facing into the wind, an overly large rain jacket flapping madly, I suddenly wondered if I could fly. Not like Superman. Not like Underdog. Just lift off and glide some distance. I leaned forward and grabbed the lower edges of my coat, holding them so the wind could fill the sides and back. I could feel the resistance and the lift, but no matter how I leaned my body or shaped the coat, I could not get off the ground. Standing straight then, I jumped into the air and flapped my arms as fast as I could, just for fun.

I did not expect the laughter that erupted behind me. I did not know there were college girls hiding under the top of the boat on the other side of the dock.

"We were hoping that would work!" one of them said.

DREAMS OF FLYING

30.

True enough, this kind of flying is all small-time stuff. Flying a rented flivver at seventy miles per hour falls perhaps somewhat short of the kind of thing one envisages in adolescent dreams; piloting in shirtsleeves and hat, instead of flying suit, helmet and goggles; and the glorious roar toned down into a rattle. It may also be perhaps less glamorous than the sort of thing that is being glorified in the newspapers and on magazine covers. I still can't beat the trains; I cannot even beat the Greyhound bus. Four hundred miles is a good daily average. It has the disadvantage furthermore that it cannot be used to impress one's best girl; when she sees you sitting in your little airplane, you are likely to appeal less to her capacity for hero worship than to her maternal instinct.

—WOLFGANG LANGEWIESCHE, *America from the Air*

31.

KFAR 042253Z 32022G32KT 10SM CLR 19/M04 A2977 RMK AO2 PK WND 32035/2237 SLP087 T01941044

32.

If I had to choose just one airplane to fly just once, for no other reason than the dance of wing and wind and talent and sky, it would not be a jet. I am not very interested in ordinary speed. It would not be a sailplane, either. I would never be satisfied with just one flight. It would not be the X-15 or the SR-71 or *Spaceship One*, even though I would sacrifice nearly anything to fly that high, to touch the edge of space where the atmosphere is so thin the rudder and ailerons are more suggestion than force.

No, the airplane I would pick for onetime flying would

be an old NASA lifting body. Probably the HL-10. No wings. Just a plump body and three vertical fins. Lift came from the shape of the whole thing. It was part of the NASA program that researched problems with reentry and guidance. It came after the x-15 and before Mercury, Gemini, or Apollo. The work done there will be the foundation for the spaceplane. But I pick this one because in one way it is so very simple, so very clear. Carried aloft by a heavy bomber, the HL-10 would be dropped from under a wing. It had a small engine and it flew supersonically, but the fuel was quickly gone and all it had to do was glide. All it could do was glide. No chance for a botched approach. No chance for a go-around or quick 360 to avoid other traffic. Keep your speed where it needs to be and hope for the dry lake bed. Just one chance to get it right.

33.

As I have said before, when you mix America, and the air, and an airplane, you get a mixture that makes an ordinary person talk about it for a long time afterwards. Here is such a mixture to talk about: how the country below me yielded and turned good. How I began to get home.

—WOLFGANG LANGEWIESCHE, *America from the Air*

The Spin

KFAR 061553Z 19005KT 10SM CLR 26/14
A3011 RMK AO2 SLP192 T02610144

Conditions at: *KFAR (FARGO, ND, US) observed 1553 UTC*
06 July 2007

Temperature: 26.1°C (79°F)

Dew point: 14.4°C (58°F) [RH = 49%]

Pressure (altimeter): 30.11 inches Hg (1019.7 mb)

[Sea-level pressure: 1019.2 mb]

Winds: from the S (190 degrees) at 6 mph (5 knots; 2.6 m/s)

Visibility: 10 or more miles (16+ km)

Ceiling: at least 12,000 feet AGL

Clouds: sky clear below 12,000 feet AGL

Weather: no significant weather observed at this time

So here is the problem.

I cannot see the altimeter, but I know we are lower than three thousand feet. The nose of the airplane is pointed straight down. The left wing is completely stalled. The right wing is partially stalled, only the small area near the tip producing any lift. And we are spinning. From my point of view, the inside of the plane looks stable while the whole planet revolves around the nose. I watch a brown field arc across the windshield, rising on the left and setting on the right, one, two, three times. I cannot see the airspeed indicator, but I know we are moving fast. In just a few seconds, if I don't do something, if I don't do the *right* something, this airplane will bury itself in the summer soil of North Dakota. In just a few seconds, I could be dead.

And here is one other bit of information. I am doing this on purpose.

In the front seat, Jake Gust is waiting to see what I will do.

Imagine the way dust curls inside the back window of a fast-moving car, or the way water curls against the downstream side of a fallen tree. The same thing happens with air moving over a wing. When the wing is level, the air flows smoothly. The shape of the wing causes the air pressure on top to be lower than the pressure on the bottom, and so the wing moves up to try to equalize the pressure. That's lift, one of the things that makes an airplane fly. But when an airplane is climbing, the wing isn't level and the air from the leading edge starts to swirl back against the wing. The steeper the climb, the higher what is called the angle of attack becomes, and the air begins to tumble and roll. Starting at the fuselage and moving outward toward the tip, lift goes away.

There are other forces at work, of course. When you see an airplane flying straight up, it has almost nothing to do with lift or the wings. It has everything to do with thrust, or momentum. A military jet has the thrust to turn it into a rocket. A stunt plane dives to pick up speed, then climbs on the momentum, like a roller coaster, until the forward motion stops.

Planes can stall at any speed. In the movie *Top Gun*, when Tom Cruise gains the advantage by pulling back on the throttle and pointing his jet's nose to the stars, causing the enemy jet to race by him, he stalls his jet. Then he recovers. Throttle forward—nose down. But in normal life, planes do not stall very often at all. Every departure angle for a commercial jet is calculated—for flight efficiency as well as passenger nerves. Every private pilot knows the stall speeds for his or her airplane and is keenly aware of staying above them. Early lessons for every pilot include what are called Power-Off Stalls, which simulate a landing, and Power-On Stalls, which simulate a takeoff. Takeoffs and landings are the danger moments. If something goes wrong, there's very little distance between the airplane and the ground.

"Full opposite rudder!" Jake says.

I press my foot on the right rudder pedal. In about half a turn, the brown field appearing in the windshield on the left but not completely disappearing on the right, the airplane stops spinning.

"Rudder neutral!" Jake says. "Now pull back!"

I even out the pedals, then pull back on the stick. Belatedly, I push the throttle forward. A thousand feet lower than where we started, the airplane is straight and level. But there is something wrong with my stomach.

"Ready to do it again?" Jake asks.

An airplane does not want to stall. Pulling back on the yoke in the little Cessna and pulling out the throttle so the thrust is next to zero, the plane begins to buffet and vibrate when the airflow begins to separate from the wings. Then a horn sounds, whiny and annoying, quietly at first, then growing louder, much louder, as the stall progresses. There's no way not to hear it. And if the approaching stall is inadvertent, there's plenty of time to take some action. Finally the airplane feels like it's running over a washboard gravel road. And then it falls. You can feel it in your gut. There is no more lift. A few seconds ago you were flying. Now you are not.

Yet the nose comes down. The angle of attack is lowered, and air can flow smoothly over the wing. The pilot pushes the throttle in, and airspeed increases. The airplane is flying again, and all is well.

At least that's the way it's supposed to happen. That's the way it happens in training all the time. But here's the kicker. When an airplane stalls, at that moment when flying turns into falling, all sorts of things can happen. And nearly all of those things are bad.

Jake and I level off just above three thousand feet. I pull the throttle back to idle, point the nose of the Decathlon up until the buzzer sounds and the whole airplane shakes. Then hard left rudder, and I will admit I do not like this feeling at all. The airplane is falling out of the sky and turning over on its side at the same time. But what I know in my head is stronger than what I fear with my gut. The nose points down, and I watch the summer prairie turn in front of me. My head goes through the routine. Full opposite rudder to stop the spin. Jake is quiet in the front seat. The spin stops, and I equalize the rudder. I know I have to add power and pull up. But in my head is another piece of information: stick forward to break the stall. I push the stick slightly forward.

"Whoa!" Jake cries over the intercom.

I can feel his hand on the yoke, pulling back.

"You almost put us in an inverted spin there," he says. "You don't want to do that."

I am quiet. At some level embarrassed at how badly I'm doing. At some level thankful as well.

"Again?" Jake asks.

An airplane can stall at any speed. When an airplane is set up for landing—full flaps, little power, straight flight—that speed can be very slow. This is good. But add a bit of turn or bank to the equation, and the stall speed goes up fast. This is because lift always moves up from the wing, but the wing may not be pointed up. If the airplane is in a 45-degree bank, then half the lift is going up, and half the lift is going to the right or the left. If an airplane stalls in this position, the lower wing will stall first. The higher wing will still be producing lift, which will cause it to rise over the lower wing. Suddenly, you are in a very bad situation.

For a small airplane, a normal approach to a landing includes two turns. The airplane begins by flying downwind, parallel to the runway. When the numbers painted on the runway are even with the pilot, power is reduced and the first bit of flaps are lowered. When the numbers are about 45 degrees behind the pilot, the plane is turned left onto what is called the base leg. The flaps are lowered some more. Finally, when the runway is even, the plane is turned to final approach. The last bit of flaps are put in here. In those two turns, however, flaps lowered and power reduced, the airplane banking to the left, stall speed can rise above the airspeed of the plane. Set up like this, the stall will nearly always cause the airplane to begin to spin. And this is one way that pilots die.

Jake and I get set up for another spin. Throttle back. Nose up. Stall horn sounding. Wings buffeting. Full left rudder. When the airplane turns over, at this moment just two people in a heavy object in the middle of the air, I smile because I've learned this feeling. I still don't like it at all, but now I recognize it. Fear has been replaced with familiarity. This is what a spin *feels* like, I think. What I knew in my brain I've now learned in my shoulders and knees.

The nose comes down, and I watch the spinning fields. Opposite rudder, and the spin is stopped. I start to pull up but hear the horn sound, so I relax on the yoke.

"Pull back!" Jake tells me.

I pull back on the stick.

"What were you doing *this* time?" he asks.

"I heard the stall horn," I say. "I was trying to be patient."

"Oh, don't worry about that," he says. "Just pull up fast. Our airspeed was up to 140. You want to recover with the minimal amount of altitude lost and the least gain in airspeed. You were putting us in accelerated stalls."

In the backseat of the Decathlon, I am shaking my head.

On the Web site for AOPA, the Aircraft Owners and Pilots Association, there is a page dedicated to the stall and spin. It begins with a truth: "Pilots who believe that aerobatic training will enable a recovery from an inadvertent spin in the traffic pattern are fooling themselves." And on my desk there is a book, lent to me by Jake, titled *Basic Aerobatics*. Chapter 14, late in the book, long after chapters on how to fly loops, slow rolls, aileron rolls, half loops, the Immelmann, the Cuban Eight, the Reverse Cuban Eight, inverted flight, the Hammerhead, and more, begins with, "At last we come to the spin, the maneuver most feared by pilots with little or no spin experience."

All through flight training, the spin is the monster in the closet, the thing that will reach out to get you if you become lazy, complacent, forgetful, or stupid. Again according to the AOPA site, stalls and spins make up 10 percent of all small-plane accidents, and nearly 14 percent of all small-plane fatal accidents. Twenty percent of small-airplane accidents are fatal, while 28 percent of stall and spin accidents are fatal.

In the old days, until 1949, every private pilot had to learn how to recover from a spin. But in that year, the requirement was taken out of the teaching. I remember asking my flight instructor why this happened, since it seemed like a good thing to know how to do. "Too many people died," he said. These days, you still learn how to recover from a stall, but you learn how to *avoid* a spin.

There is value to knowing the shape of a problem. In all likelihood, unless I'm in training, I will never stall an airplane on purpose. But I know what causes it, what it feels like when it appears, and how to get out of one quickly. I have no intention of spinning an aircraft, either. But now I know what's waiting in that corner.

If a spin sneaks up on me and I'm in the landing pattern, there isn't enough air between me and the ground to recover.

Like nearly every other "pilot error" accident, it will be my own damn fault for letting the airplane get in front of me. But spins can happen anytime during maneuvering—when the pilot is actually flying instead of simply pointing in a direction and enjoying the view. If the monster appears and there is some room between me and the wheat, I know what to do.

One more time. Jake holds onto bars by his shoulders, and I have the airplane. Throttle back. Nose up. Rudder. Stick. Opposite rudder. Pull back. Throttle forward. It isn't pretty at all, but we're straight and level again, and only eight hundred feet lower than where we started.

"You've been taught," Jake says, "that all spins are bad."

"Yes, I have," I say.

I can see his head nod up and down. Outside the windows, the sunlight is bright on the fields, the midsummer crops half-height and green. Section roads mark the land, while small rivers seem to dance and make fun of the lines. I can see silver grain bins, cars, trucks, a train moving northwestward, and in the distance another small airplane flying west.

We turn to the east, back toward Jake and Barb's farm. We've only been flying an hour, but we both have things to do.

"You have anything left back there?" he asks me.

"Of course," I say.

Then, only because it's fun, we fly a loop.

The World Record

Part One

KISN 181752Z VRB05KT 10SM CLR 28/06 A2995 RMK A02
ALP134 T02830061 10289 20100 58014

There ought to be music.
Big music.
Fast music.
Heavy on drums and bass.
Lots of brass. Trumpet screamers. Trombones.
Exciting, fast, electric. Sexy as hell.
Think Bill Chase, Maynard Ferguson, Buddy Rich, maybe Tower of Power or Blood, Sweat, and Tears.
Something like a James Bond theme or "Mission Impossible." Only better. Faster. Double forte. Double time.
This is *world* record time.
This is world *speed* record time.
A world aviation speed record for "Speed Over a Recognized Course."

And I am the pilot.
If only I could stop laughing.

In Williston, North Dakota, there is a message on my cell phone. A television crew wants to talk with me. Already, back in Fargo, the story has been in the newspaper and on the radio. "Local man hopes to set world speed record." It has a certain ring to it. No one seems to notice, or care, that the plane I am flying is very slow. A Cessna 152. A single-engine trainer—the plane I learned to fly in. It has more hours on the airframe than I really want to know. Tail number: November Five Three Two Nine Bravo. Top speed: 110 knots (127 miles) per hour.

Yes, at one level this whole thing is a lark. But it's also real, and official, and certified. It's not quite the Collier Trophy, which went to Chuck Yeager in 1947 for breaking the sound barrier, to the *Spaceship One* team in 2004, and more recently to the developers of the F-22 Raptor. And it's not quite the Wright Brothers Memorial Trophy, which is given to people like Eugene Cernan, the last person to walk on the moon. But at the National Aeronautic Association (NAA, the oldest aviation organization in the United States and the official aviation record keeper for the country) there is a category—for both national and world titles—called "Speed Over a Recognized Course." What this means is you set a course that can be observed by Air Traffic Control, and then you try to be the fastest person to fly that route in a specific class of airplane. And if there is no record before you, then you can set the mark. As long as your average speed, including stops, is faster than the stall speed of the airplane, then your name goes on the important plaques and certificates. You get invited to a fancy dinner in Washington DC. The world thinks you are special.

As long as the average speed is higher than the speed at which the airplane falls out of the sky, you could stop for cheeseburgers, double orders of fries, and extrathick shakes. And you could even get a bit huffy if the cook is slow because you are, after all, setting a world speed record.

Two Nine Bravo is hardly a speed machine. But looking at the NAA Web site, just curious about records in my own back-yard, I discovered there was no record, no record at all, for the fastest flight across North Dakota. None. Zip. Nothing. There was a record for a round-trip flight from Fargo to Bis-marck and back, but otherwise the state seemed wide open. No way, I thought. Then, I thought, of course. Of course, this could be done. Of course, this *had* to be done. And, of course, *I* had to be the one to do it. A few phone calls and e-mails later it was clear: I could set a world speed record in an airplane often passed by cars on the highway.

Williston, North Dakota, is a town of just over twelve thousand people on the banks of the Missouri River in the northwest corner of the state. There's a small airport on the northwest side of the city, and northwest of the airport there is a VOR, a radio beacon used for aircraft navigation. Air traf-fic controllers at the Salt Lake Center can "see" the VOR and the transponders of the airplanes that are near it. This VOR is why I am here. It's the westernmost in the state, and I need Air Traffic Control to mark the time I pass over it, heading east, to set the official start time of my record.

From Williston, the plan is to fly to Bismarck, where I will have to make a decision. Stop for gas, or bank left and head for Fargo. Three hundred and fifty-nine miles over Badlands and rivers and prairie, over Lake Sakakawea and then the Red River valley. No wind. This is just the range of a 152. If I pass by Bismarck, I could make it to Fargo with gas to spare. If I pass by Bismarck, I could run out before the runway. There are a lot of variables. Temperature. Rpm setting. Luck of the draw.

The news crew sets up by the airplane. The pretty blonde reporter is the anchor for the local evening news. The cameraman likes dumb jokes. They want to know why I am doing this, why setting a world record is important. I tell them that records are important because they set an edge, a border, a mark by which we judge ourselves. I tell them that it doesn't really matter if we're talking about eating hot dogs or setting speed records; once there is a number, someone else will want to do more. This record, I say, is really an invitation to other pilots: here is the mark; let's see if you can go faster. What I don't tell them is that I'm really just goofing off.

"Williston Traffic, Cessna Five Three Two Nine Bravo is on the ramp, taxiing to the end of runway one-one, Williston."

There is no reply. There is no control tower at Williston, so the radio routine is pretty simple. It's called self-announcing. You begin with the name of the airport, state what you're doing, and end with the name of the airport. Other airplanes in the area will hear you, and, if everything works, you will avoid an unpleasant meeting.

"Williston Traffic, Cessna Five Three Two Nine Bravo is taxiing onto one-one for takeoff, Williston."

Nothing. I look down the runway. Southeast. That's my direction. Toward Bismarck. Toward Fargo. Toward fame!

THE WORLD RECORD

But first I have to fly the other direction, to find the VOR, to call Salt Lake Center.

"Williston Traffic, Cessna Five Three Two Nine Bravo is rolling on one-one, Williston."

The little plane rolls beautifully down the runway, and I'd swear it lifts itself into the afternoon air. I can see the news crew still on the ramp, taking video of my departure. I wait until I'm over them, then just to show off put the plane in a dramatic bank to the left.

There ought to be music. Think Tchaikovsky. Think John Williams. *The 1812. Star Wars. Indiana Jones.*

Thanks to Einstein, we know that speed and position are relative, given the speed and position of the observer, although the speed of light remains a constant. Yet we are obsessed with speed. How fast can I run the hundred-yard dash? How fast is the processor in my computer? How quickly will my car get to sixty miles per hour? We *desire* speed. We spend lifetimes and then generations getting faster. A tomato that ripens in half a season. A faster-dissolving tablet to get the medicine in our blood. And with speed as the goal, racing becomes the dance. Who will be the first to fill in the blank? Who will fill the blank the fastest?

The first air race was the Grande Semaine d'Aviation in Reims, France, in 1909. What was called the James Gordon Bennett Trophy was won by American Glenn Curtiss, who blazed across the sky at 46.5 miles per hour and set the first international airspeed record. Then came the Schneider Trophy, officially the Coupe d'Aviation Maritime Jacques Schneider, for seaplane racing. In the United States, 1921 saw the start of the National Air Meets, which became the National

Air Races. Then came the Women's Air Derby, the Cleveland Air Races, and the All-Woman Transcontinental Air Race. In 1964, a rancher and racing pilot named Bill Stead started the Reno Air Races, which became the National Championship Air Races. The Red Bull Energy Drink company has its own series, held all over the world. Hundreds of thousands of people watch the challenge of speed and sky.

Yet racing isn't simple. The Reno races look like the Indy 500, multiple airplanes flying around an oval circuit, while the Red Bull races are single-plane events, flying between pylons and accomplishing required moves in the intervals—all against the clock. In other words, you can be faster than the guy flying next to you. Or you can be faster than everyone else in the sky.

Three hundred and fifty-nine miles. The space shuttle covers this trek in one minute and twenty seconds. The X-15 in four minutes flat. A fast 747 could make the leap in thirty-eight minutes. The flight plan for Two Nine Bravo shows a little more than four hours.

A short distance north and west of Williston, the Dakota prairie under the July sun is brown and hard grassland. The white VOR building with the cone on top is as conspicuous as the obelisk in *2001: A Space Odyssey*. Ten minutes off the ground, it's time for me to check in.

"Salt Lake Center, Cessna Five Three Two Nine Bravo . . ."

"Cessna Five Three Two Nine Bravo, go ahead."

"Have request," I say. "You should have been briefed about marking my time crossing the Williston VOR today?"

"November Five Three Two Nine Bravo, roger. Do you

want a code, or do you want to just give me a call me when you cross the VOR?"

"Well, I'm coming up on it here. You can tell me one way or the other."

"November Two Nine Bravo, squawk four zero four one, please."

"Four zero four one, Two Nine Bravo," I reply.

"November Two Nine Bravo, radar contact. Two and a half miles southeast of the VOR, three thousand five hundred, Williston altimeter two niner niner five."

"Thank you very much," I say.

"You want me to record the time when you turn east over the VOR—is that correct?" the controller asks.

"That is correct."

"November Two Nine Bravo, roger. I'll let you know."

What I imagine is the lightning streak, the fast dive toward the ground, the hard bank around a corner, the kind of flying you see in the movies. There should be some farm kids playing on a farmstead, and they should whisper "Golly" to themselves as I go by. Their dog should bark in both amazement and alarm. But this is a Cessna 152. Two and a half miles. Yep. Okay.

Now two and a quarter miles. Way to go.

I'm scooting forward in my seat, trying to urge just a little more speed out of the airplane. Patience, I think to myself. Two miles to go.

Finally, I pass the VOR on the north side and begin a turn to the left.

Salt Lake Center comes on the radio immediately.

"November Two Nine Bravo, I show you over the VOR at one eight two six."

"Thank you very much. Have a good day," I say.

"November Two Nine Bravo, you can squawk VFR now."

I have been dismissed by Salt Lake Center.

The race is on!

Speed is everything.

In an airplane, speed is what keeps you in the sky. Every climb, every turn, every glide, every stall is defined by a speed. They are called v-speeds and measured in KIAS, or knots indicated airspeed. Ground speed doesn't keep you flying. The speed of the air over your wings defines what you can do, and the airspeed indicator gives you the number. In the 152, Vr is when you can rotate, or lift the nose toward the sky, and it's 50 knots. Vx is the definition of the maximum climb angle: 55 knots. Vy is the best climb rate: 67 knots. Va is normal maneuvering speed: 104 knots. Vfe is the maximum speed you can have the flaps extended: 85 knots. Vno is the normal maximum speed in smooth air: 111 knots. Vne is the speed you never exceed, unless you want your wings to land someplace else: 149 knots. Vso is the stall speed in a landing configuration, flaps extended: 35 knots.

Every airplane is different. Vne for a Twin Otter is 202 knots. Vne for a 747 is Mach 0.92. These are the speeds you memorize. They're not very interesting, but they keep you alive.

Then there are the other speeds, the ones that are interesting, the ones we use for our dreams and our passions, the ones we use to say who we are. On the Web, a Google search that took 0.19 seconds tells me that:

THE WORLD RECORD

On October 15, 1997, British Royal Air Force pilot Andy Green set the world land speed record at 763 miles per hour, in the jet-driven ThrustSSC. He became the first person to break the sound barrier in a land vehicle.

On September 5, 2006, Chris Carr set the motorcycle land speed record at 350 mph.

The fastest unmanned rocket sled went 6,416 mph in 2003.

The fastest manned rocket sled went 635 mph in 1954.

The fastest magnetic levitation train went 361 mph in 2003.

The fastest wheeled train went 357 mph in 2007.

The fastest unmanned air-breathing aircraft, the Boeing X-43A scramjet, went 7,000 mph in 2004.

The fastest manned air-breathing aircraft, the SR-71 Blackbird, went 2,194 mph in 1976.

The list keeps going.

The fastest rocket-powered aircraft was the X-15 at 4,510 mph.

The fastest propeller-driven aircraft, the Tupolev Tu-114, went 541 mph.

The fastest piston-engine propeller aircraft, a Grumman F8F Bearcat, went 528 mph.

The fastest helicopter was the Westland Lynx 800 at 249 mph.

The fastest human-powered aircraft, the MIT Monarch B, was flown by Frank Scarabino on the first of May in 1984, and reached a top speed of 19.8 miles per hour.

The water speed record is 317 miles per hour.

The underwater speed record is 38 miles per hour.

The record for an unmanned spacecraft, the Heliois 2 probe, is 157,078 mph.

The record for a manned spacecraft is held by *Apollo 10* at 24,790 mph.

The world, and then the whole universe, can be expressed in terms of speed. If one meter per second becomes a constant for measuring magnitude, then the speed of a garden snail is 0.013 m/s, or 1×10^{-2}. The average speed of continental drift is 0.3×10^{-9} to 3×10^{-9}. The typical speed of a Moreton wave across the surface of the sun is 1×10^6 or 1,000,000 m/s. The speed of my hair is 4.8×10^{-9}.

Think *Peter Gunn*. Think the theme from *Hawaii Five-O*.

There is a problem with flying in clear air on a sunny summer afternoon. The sunshine heats the earth, the earth heats the air, and by afternoon thermals rise and give birth to the soft white cotton-ball clouds everyone loves. If you are the pilot of a sailplane, you live for each thermal, each chance to rise higher into the sky. But if you're flying a little prop job like the 152, each thermal is a bump and a jolt. It's good form to hold a steady altitude, but the ride pushes you up, and then doesn't, and then pushes you up again. It's not the kind of turbulence that would make you afraid. It's more like an old and poorly maintained gravel road, with ruts. After a while you can feel your teeth coming loose.

Two Nine Bravo has only one radio, so I use my cell phone to open the flight plan.

"Welcome to Lockheed Martin Flight Service. This is Princeton, Minnesota."

"Hi," I say. "I need to activate a flight plan, please. This is Cessna Five Three Two Nine Bravo."

"November Five Two Three Niner Bravo. Is that close, sir?"

"Five Three Two Nine Bravo," I repeat, slowly.

"Five Three Three Nine Bravo."

"No . . . Five Three Two Nine."

"Five Three Two Nine."

"Yes."

"Okay, that's off of Williston. Is that correct, sir?"

Lord, I think.

"Yes, it is."

"Just a second here. Okay . . . I'll activate at this time, sir, and monitor AWOS for the current altimeter. Is there anything else I can help you with, sir?"

Of course, what I want to tell him is I'm setting a record, that I'm flying fast, that I need him to clear the skies for the lightning streak that is me, but I do not. There is a seagull up here, at my altitude and in front of me. I'd swear it is flying faster.

"That'll do it," I say.

"Okay, sir, you have a good day."

Then the radio comes back to life.

"Williston Traffic, maintenance vehicle entering two-nine-one-one, Williston."

A few moments later, "Maintenance vehicle clear of two-nine-one-one, Williston."

Yes. I am blistering across the sky.

There are races against another person, and there are races against time. Then there are the races just to see if you can do it. Just to see if you can survive.

One of these is called the Race to the Clouds, the Pikes Peak International Hill Climb. Eighteen different divisions of race car, motorcycle, and truck begin at 9,402 feet above sea level, nearly 6,000 feet higher than I am right now behind the yoke of Two Nine Bravo, and they race twelve and a half miles, half paved and half gravel, to a finish at 14,110 feet. A climb of 4,708 feet, road grades of 10 percent, hairpin turns with no barriers before the launch into canyon voids if a mistake is made or attention wanders. A race past places with names like Horseshoe, Gayler's Straits, Brown Bush Corner, Big Spring, Heitman's Hill, Gilly's Corner, Tin Barn, Sump, Ragged Edge, Double Cut, Devil's Playground, Bottomless Pit, Boulder Park, and Summit. People crash and people die on the way toward being the fastest up the hill.

Then there is Le Mans, the twenty-four-hour endurance race with the dramatic start where drivers line up across the track from their cars. When the French tricolor flag is waved it's a footrace for the ignition, and this fact alone is why Porsche ignition switches are on the left of the steering wheel. This was also the first race where the winning driver sprayed champagne instead of drinking it.

Three thousand feet above sea level, I am smiling as Two Nine Bravo crosses the Missouri River. The ignition switch in this Cessna is on the left side of the yoke. I doubt anyone will be spraying champagne, but over the water the thermals have evened out and the air is smooth and fast. When I get to the far side, however, steep bluffs and ravines, grasslands and approaching buttes, the bumps come back. There is no doubt about my seat belt. This is work, I say to myself. Four hours of this ahead of me. At Le Mans, no driver is allowed to drive more than four hours, although in the past this was not always the case. The Pikes Peak International Hill Climb takes between ten and twenty minutes. It's not as easy to name pockets of air as it is to name a dramatic curve in a mountain roadway, but I begin to put together a list. Scott's Spleen. Scott's Kidney. Scott's Neck against the Shoulder Belt. Scott's Coffee.

By definition, a record is impressive. First man on the moon: Neil Armstrong. First solo across the Atlantic: Charles Lindbergh. First to break the sound barrier: Chuck Yeager. But there is a line of buttes up ahead, and my flight path seems to take me between two of them. I need to pay attention to what I am doing.

One hundred and thirteen nautical miles away from Bismarck, my ground speed is 76 knots. My airspeed is about 85 knots. The GPS says I'm still an hour thirty from the airport, from the decision I will need to make about fuel. The thermals are rising so strong it's hard to keep the airplane down, so I throttle back just to keep from rocketing into the stratosphere. Every time I enter the shadow of a cloud the airplane starts going up, which all things considered is a good thing.

Lake Sakakawea is off to my left. A beautiful deep blue and green. Not a single boat that I can see from here. A shoreline untroubled by industry or tourist marinas, the lake winds like the wide river it really is. Green, in a way that is not even close to the color of the lake, and then brown, the grassland passes below me. Farmsteads. Oil rigs. The weathered gray shells of long-abandoned homes. Dirt roads, just two parallel wheel tracks, leading from one vague somewhere to one vague somewhere else. Sagebrush. Beautiful country. As I pass the small range of buttes, their rise in elevation brings them closer to Two Nine Bravo, and I once again get a sensation of speed, the cuts and draws and ravines as quickly out of view as in. Somewhere off toward the right horizon is the town of Dickenson, and then Medora. The Badlands. Teddy Roosevelt National Park. History.

A bit of smooth air, and then the thermals come back. I am wrestling this airplane, and loving every moment, over the high desert of North Dakota on a beautiful summer afternoon in July, even though I have to force myself to relax sometimes, sitting all scrunched up because of the work of the ride.

Think Aaron Copland. *Rodeo.*

An odd thing about flying, at least my type of flying, low and slow, touring and exploring in the oldest and best sense of the words, is that you think a lot about landing. On the ground, you can't wait to get into the air. You can't wait for that change in perspective, that every-time-fresh reordering of how one place fits with another. But once in the air, you imagine a thousand landings. Part of this is safety. Somewhere early in flight lessons you learn that airplane engines can, and sometimes do, quit without warning. There can be fire from fuel, and fire from the electrical system. You can run out of gas, or something could break. There are a thousand reasons you might need to get down fast. So you spend your time looking at the ground, thinking, "I can land there, or there, or there . . ." But there is another reason a pilot's mind can turn toward landing. The earth itself is an invitation.

Every brown bit of grassland that seems to level, every grown-over but still visible dirt road is an invitation to lower the flaps, pull back the throttle, settle the airplane out of the sky. There is something magical about arriving this way, as if the angels have let you down to visit. Time moves at some other pace as you linger, perhaps talk with a rancher, perhaps fish in some stream. The miles between you and the nearest good water, the nearest food, the nearest shelter are irrelevant. You don't have to hike or drive the miles. The distance is easy, as is the distance beyond. If you remove the burden of distance, then the idea of *here* becomes intimate and special. The bush pilot who lands on a sliver of a river gravel bar, or in some tight mountain pasture graded toward smooth, or the floatplane pilot who finds a lake more remote than the one before—they are hearing the same call. To find an expression of *here* that can fill the heart.

Ninety nautical miles and seventy minutes from Bismarck. So many pretty ravines. These thermals are killing me. Some of the cloud shapes, however, are really fantastic. Lion heads. Cornucopias. Swirls and flats. I start humming to myself. The "*William Tell* Overture." Any other music that's exciting and fast. I can't hum worth a damn. Do I feel like this is a race? Yes. Absolutely. This isn't just flying. This is racing. This is getting there as fast as I can. At a whopping 82.2 knots. Oh, please give me some smooth air.

I may have a problem. I don't know why, but fuel seems to be coming out of the left tank faster than it's coming out of the right. Oil pressure looks good, oil temperature looks good, suction looks good. All the gauges are fine. The radio is fine. The GPS is fine. But the two fuel gauges do not match. The left tank reads about seven gallons, the needle bumping and dancing with each bump in the air. The right tank still reads full at twelve, the needle pinned against the side.

This could be no problem at all. I am flying in uneven air—there is no good reason the tanks would drain at the same speed. But if both gauges were reading the same, I would feel better about how much fuel I have and not wonder if one is stuck, if there is a problem with the vent, if I should assume there is enough to keep me flying.

Just past the town of Hazen, I see a small airstrip, the single runway in the short distance to my left. KHZE. Mercer County Regional. In town, the subdivisions are new and sparkling. I can see a lot of new construction. Here by the airport, the land is farmed for crops, each plant a different color, each color a different stripe in the mosaic. Dark green, light brown, light green, yellow.

I change the radio over to the Bismarck Approach frequency, and as if on cue I hear an announcement.

"Bismarck ATIS, Mike is now current. Altimeter two niner niner seven."

I check my altimeter and make a small adjustment, and try to urge the plane a bit faster through the sky. This is the moment of decision. This is when I need to decide if I am going to turn left, head toward Fargo, and pray that I've got the fuel to get there, or keep on straight to Bismarck, land, gas up as fast as lightning, and get back into the sky.

Just past Mercer County Regional, my GPS says I am 191.6 nautical miles from Fargo. It says I am 110.3 nautical miles from the Williston VOR. I could have as much as seventeen gallons of fuel left in the wings. I could have less if something isn't working right. If I have seventeen, I can fly to Fargo and linger when I get there. If I have less, in simple terms, I cannot.

On the radio, I listen as a plane owned by the Department

of the Interior asks to shoot a missed approach in Mandan (the town next to Bismarck), then turn back and land in Bismarck. Bismarck Approach gives its approval.

Turn or land? I wonder. Turn or land? I am setting a world speed record! Turn or land?

A bump inside a thermal shoves me hard against the seat belts, but the clouds are thinning and the air is growing quieter. I am 33.5 nautical miles northwest of the Bismarck airport, passing an open strip mine for coal. I can see the ribbon of the Missouri River off to my left, a gunmetal blue in the afternoon sun. I can see the buttes and rises of western North Dakota off to my right. The farmland below me is rich and lush. If I turn, I will spend the next two hours staring at the fuel gauges, apprehensive and worried. If I land, however, I will worry about my time. All I have to do is stay faster than the stall speed of the airplane. But my in-my-head math skills are not very good. How long can I stay on the ground before my *average* speed falls below stall speed? There is a part of me that knows this whole thing is silly—a world aviation speed record in a Cessna 152—but there is another part of me, growing with each moment, that wants my time to be real, or at least respectable. Speed, I have decided, matters.

"Good afternoon, Bismarck, Cirrus One Nine Charlie, level six point five, with Mike, request."

Another airplane, somewhere ahead of me, is on the radio.

"Cirrus One Nine Charlie, Bismarck Approach. Say your request."

"Sir, if we can fly the DME arc and then do the ILS approach to runway one-three."

"Cirrus One Nine Charlie, cleared for the seventeen-mile arc, northeast, expect ILS runway one-three approach, maintain VFR."

"Maintain VFR," the pilot says. But then he continues: "If you guys have time, can you kinda watch me on vectors a little bit? If not, I'll do it on my own nav, but if you could keep an eye on me I'd appreciate it."

"Well, that's what we're doing," Approach replies. "Watching ya."

"Thanks a lot."

Yes, I think, there are people in the tower at Bismarck, people in the tower in Fargo, people in Salt Lake City and people in Minneapolis who can keep an eye on us all. But turn or land? They can't answer that one. And if I make the wrong decision, all they can do is watch, and then call for rescue.

Yes, think the opening to Beethoven's Fifth Symphony.

I look out the window. Land, I say. Get this thing on the ground and then get it back up in the sky. I'd rather miss the record because I was too slow than miss the record because I was planted with the soybeans. I turn the radio to the frequency of the FBO (fixed base operator) in Bismarck.

"Executive Air Taxi, Cessna Five Three Two Nine Bravo."

Nothing.

I wait a few minutes and then try again.

"Executive Air Taxi, Cessna Five Three Two Nine Bravo."

Nothing. I am not yet in range.

Closer, I think. Closer. The music builds. Think Ravel's *Boléro*.

A few moments later: "Executive Air Taxi, Cessna Five Three Two Nine Bravo."

"Two Nine Bravo, Executive Air. Go ahead."

Oh joy!

"I'm about eighteen minutes out," I say, "and when I get there, I'm going to need the fastest fuel stop for a little 152 we've ever seen."

"Okay, we'll be standing by."

In motor racing, the pit stop is an art and an adventure all of its own. And while credit should go to the 1963 Daytona 500 and Wood Brothers Racing for inventing the specialized dance we now think is normal, nowhere is the pit stop more elegant or more refined than at the Indianapolis 500, "The Greatest Spectacle in Racing."

We know the race, and we know the drivers' names. They are American Lore, and American Heroes. Wally Dallenbach. Johnny Rutherford. Tom Sneva. Bobby Unser. A. J. Foyt. Rick Mears. Michael Andretti. Bobby Rahal. Mario Andretti. Al Unser Jr. But has anyone ever heard of Dave Klym, Steve Roby, Paul Leffler, Chuck Sprague, Owen Snyder, Darren Russell, Matt Jonsson, or Rick Rinaman? These are the chief mechanics, the guys who build the cars, repair the cars, tweak the cars, love the cars. And these are the guys who put together the team that can leap a wall and in only seconds get the race car fueled and tires changed.

It is its own ballet, filled with crashes and miscues as well as the art of a human body on task. And every year, before the day of the actual race, there is the McDonald's Pit Stop Challenge. The winning team makes fifty thousand dollars. In 1977 Dave Klym's team won with a pit time of 15.09 seconds. In 1989 Owen Snyder's team won at 14.716 seconds. In 1994 Kyle Moyer's team won in 12.867 seconds. In 2007

Rick Rinaman's team won with a flabbergasting 8.335 seconds, in front of Matt Monsson's team, which posted a time of 8.888 seconds. Yet none of these times comes even close to 1976, when during the race, which became the shortest Indy 500 ever because of rain, Bobby Unser completed a pit stop in 4 seconds.

I cannot say I am expecting this kind of speed. On the ground, nothing should be done quickly with an airplane. But I have been here before. Early this morning, when the sky was still an indigo blue and fog still filled each low fold in the landscape, I stood at the desk of Executive Air Taxi on my way out to Williston.

"I may be here this afternoon," I said. "And I may not. I really don't know yet. But I'm doing this speed-record thing. So if you see me, we need to make it really fast."

The ladies at the desk smiled and nodded at me. I'm sure they saw the plane and figured I was nuts.

No problem, they said.

"Bismarck Approach, Cessna Five Three Two Nine Bravo is twenty-four miles out to the northwest, coming in at thirty-seven hundred feet, full stop."

"Cessna Five Three Two Nine Bravo, Bismarck Approach, squawk zero three four one."

"Zero three four one, Two Nine Bravo."

"Two Nine Bravo, did you get Mike for the ATIS yet?"

"Yes, I did, thank you."

"Two Nine Bravo, radar contact, twenty-three northwest of the airport. Make straight in for runway one-three."

"Straight to one-three. Thank you, Two Nine Bravo."

Straight in. I like the sound of that. Fast. No turns, no

waiting. Straight in. As much as I wish I was flying with the approach speed of the space shuttle, I am not. I can see the homes that front the Missouri River, the docks and the boats tied up there. I can see the traffic on the highways. I can see the color of the stoplights, and I can wait to watch them change. I can see an old man walking a very small dog. I can watch them both for some time.

Think "Funeral March of a Marionette," which was the theme from *Alfred Hitchcock Presents*.

Then the airport is in sight.

"Cessna Two Nine Bravo, contact tower on one one eight point three."

"Going to tower, Two Nine Bravo. Thank you." I change the frequency on the radio. "Bismarck Tower, Cessna Five Three Two Nine Bravo is eight miles to the northwest at thirty-two hundred feet, coming in for a full stop."

"Cessna Five Three Two Nine Bravo, Bismarck Tower, make straight in."

"Will do, Two Nine Bravo."

Then the other airplane comes back on the radio.

"Bismarck Approach, November Seven Six One, missed approach over at Mandan."

"Seven Six One, Bismarck Tower, understand inbound, landing Bismarck?"

"Seven Six One, affirmative."

"November Seven Six One, roger. Fly heading of zero four zero to follow traffic just north of I-94 on a straight in to one-three."

"Seven Six One, right to zero four zero, we'll plan number two for one-three."

I cannot say why, but suddenly I am filled with energy.

I'm landing first. This guy has to wait for me! A world aviation speed record! And then,

"Cessna Two Nine Bravo, runway one-three, clear to land."

"Clear to land, Two Nine Bravo. Thank you."

Six One is told my position, but reports "no joy." He can't see me. Tower tells him to continue on his heading and keep looking, then a few moments later tells him to turn and head straight in behind me. My smile is huge.

Throttle back. Carb heat. Ten percent flaps. Runway numbers fixed in my window. Speed at 90, then 80, then 70. More flaps. Engine to idle. I cross the numbers and flare, and the stall horn begins to whine just as my wheels touch down. Perfect. Exactly two hours and twenty-eight seconds since Salt Lake Center said go.

Bismarck Tower comes on the radio. "Two Nine Bravo, turn right Charlie three, and taxi to parking."

"Will do, Two Nine Bravo."

I turn right off the runway and taxi toward the FBO. The line guys are already outside, waving their yellow batons, directing me toward parking. The fuel truck is running, its rooftop lights flashing. When I get in place and the propeller stops, they are damn fast. One guy connects the ground wire, another places a stepladder near a wing and hauls the fuel line to the top. A third even comes to my door and opens it for me as I try to disconnect the seat belts.

"You guys are good," I say.

He smiles at me. I walk to the lobby, each step a type of relearning after the thermals, and inside I have a small cup of coffee. There is a part of me that really does want to linger, to order the cheeseburger, the extra order of fries, the extrathick shake. But, honestly, I have this need to get going. One of the line guys literally runs the fuel ticket to the counter, where one of the women rings it up. I sign the receipt, and at the last minute decide to stop in the bathroom. When I come out, a line guy is holding the lobby door open for me. He walks me to the plane, and we talk about fuel and oil. I explain what I'm doing, and he laughs. "Sounds like fun!" he says. When I bend myself back into the airplane and attach the seat belts, he pats the side of the plane and wishes me luck. I close the door. One more leg—Bismarck to Fargo. One more landing.

Think of the theme to *Bridge on the River Kwai*.

Part Two

KBIS 182052Z 17014G19KT 10SM FEW060 29/13 A2996 RMK AO2 SLP138 T02890128 56014

In the entire database of the National Aeronautics Association, there are only ten records held by a Cessna 152. They are:

Dinard to St. Peter, 114.66 mph, David O'Byrne, UK, 1985.
Duluth to Oshkosh, 106.75 mph, Stanley Mick, USA, 1993.
Fairbanks to Oshkosh, 27.83 mph, Stanley Mick, USA, 1993 (set before there was a minimum speed requirement).
Lincoln to Sioux Falls, 150.48 mph, Robert Carlisle and Jon Howser, USA, 1978.
Minot to Duluth, 93.57 mph, Stanley Mick, USA, 1993.
New York to Martha's Vineyard, 93.12 mph, Phil Scott, USA, 1995.

Oshkosh to Van Nuys, 60.45 mph, Jennifer Riley, USA, 1991.

St. Louis to South Bend, 124.4 mph, Stanley Mick, USA, 1992.

Topeka to St. Louis, 128.88 mph, Stanley Mick, USA, 1992.

Toronto to Montreal, 109.53 mph, Bernard Runstedler, Canada, 1995.

There are fifteen records for the Cessna 150, essentially the same airplane, just an older model (Bloemfontein, South Africa, to Pretoria, South Africa, 125.95 mph, Hans Schwebel, Germany, 2006; Blenheim to Invergargill, 89.61 mph, John Nickolas Darragh Matheson and Wayne Matheson, New Zealand, 2002; Santa Anna, California, to Bangor, Maine, 91.74 mph, James Nelson, USA, 1976), and a grand total of twenty-seven records, of any type at all, that begin or end in North Dakota. These include a balloon-duration record of twenty-three hours and twelve records for fastest climb to altitude, each accomplished by a Rockwell International B1-B bomber flying out of the Minot Air Force Base.

Strapped in again to the left seat in Two Nine Bravo, these records carry some weight as I finish the preflight, open the window, and yell, "Clear!" No reply, so I turn the key, the engine fires, and then that wonderful dip of the nose as the propeller begins to bite the air and you have to press on the brakes to keep from rolling.

I tune the radio to the ATIS. "Bismarck airport information Mike, one niner five zero Zulu observation, winds one six zero eight, gusts one six, visibility one zero, clear, temp is two eight, dew point one one, altimeter two niner niner seven, visual-approach runway one-three in use, advise on initial contact you have ATIS information Mike."

I look around the cabin. A small habit, just wondering what I haven't noticed, haven't done, haven't remembered. Then I dial in a new frequency on the radio. It's time to nail this thing. It's time to join that list, to set a world record for aviation speed.

Think of the theme to *Rawhide*. Think of *The Blues Brothers*. I key the mic.

"Bismarck Ground, Cessna Five Three Two Nine Bravo is on the ramp, ready to go, departing to the east, going to Fargo at or below three thousand, information Mike."

"Airplane calling Bismarck," a controller replies, sounding weary, "Bismarck Ground frequency is one two one point nine."

Oh, great! Wrong frequency. I just called Bismarck Tower instead of Bismarck Ground. It's not a big mistake, but it does declare to everyone in radio range that at some level I am an idiot.

I change the radio again.

"Bismarck Ground," I say, "Cessna Five Three Two Nine Bravo is at the ramp heading to Fargo, information Mike, at or below three thousand."

"Cessna Five Three Two Nine Bravo, Bismarck Ground. Taxi to runway one-three via taxiway Charlie."

"Going to one-three, Two Nine Bravo. Thank you."

I push in the throttle, and the airplane leaves the parking area, turns left onto the taxiway. At the end of the runway, the final preflight checks, the engine run-up, and then I'm ready to go. Ready to fly. Ready to become a line of computer script in someone's database.

"Bismarck Tower, Cessna Five Three Two Nine Bravo is at runway one-three, ready to go!"

"Cessna Five Three Two Nine Bravo, Bismarck Tower. Proceed on course, cleared for takeoff."

The mighty engine roars!

Two Nine Bravo races down one more runway, and once again we are airborne, turning east, the capital of North Dakota falling away behind us. So too the shopping centers, the university, the neighborhoods and businesses. Think of the theme to *Jonny Quest*.

There's a dead fly on the dash. Just saw it flopping about in the air from a vent. Scared the life out of me. At first, it looked like something outside, like something coming off from underneath the cowling. The first signs of a prop or engine disintegrating. But it's just a fly. A dead fly.

I-94 is off to my left. Trucks and cars moving both directions, steady but nowhere near congested. I can follow this road all the way home. Clouds and thermals again. Two more hours of the roller coaster. Two more hours of wrestling an airplane and the sky. On my GPS I can read the names of lakes and towns as they pass beside or underneath me. Long Lake is off to my right. Alkaline Lake is in the short distance ahead.

The clouds are thinning, and the sun is behind me now. The wind is an easy breeze. It's a wonderful and beautiful day for flying. I look out my window and down to the highway. A semitruck, bright-red cab and white trailer, is on the eastbound lane beside me. Two motorcycles race toward the west. Off to the south, green farmlands recede toward the horizon. It's too early for harvest, and long past planting.

There are no tractors, no combines in the fields. This is picture-postcard time. This is the time when farmers inhale.

I look out my window again. There is that semi. Still right beside me. Okay, I think. Here comes the test. Am I passing cars and trucks on the road, or are they passing me? I watch the truck. It's a dead heat. No, no, no, I whisper. I am setting a world speed record! I push in the throttle a bit. I gain some ground, or some air, or something. Yes! I say out loud. I am slightly faster than an eighteen-wheel truck! Not much. But still, faster. Think "Flight of the Bumblebee." The GPS says I'm doing 75 knots.

Coming up on the towns of Driscoll, Steele, and Dawson, four thousand feet above sea level, the dead fly gets caught in the vent blast and flies by my head at what seems like Mach 2. I have to duck to avoid injury. Down on the highway, that semi is just a bit behind my shoulder. I have to turn my head to see him. Ha! I think. I've got the afterburners lit, the supercharger going. The truck driver has no idea, but we are racing and I am ahead.

Alkaline Lake is south of Dawson, and south of Alkaline is Lake Isabell, round and blue-green in the afternoon sunlight. Two Hobie Cat sailboats mirror each other as they cross, no doubt racing each other, and a Jet Ski pulls a tube. I watch as the Jet Ski cracks the whip and sends the tube rider bouncing and tumbling over the lake surface until the surface breaks and the splash is huge.

An hour thirty away from home. An hour thirty until this race is over. Just passed Tappen on the way to Medina. Watching I-29 cut through fields and small lakes. Even at altitude, huge bugs explode on the windshield. Every good racing vehicle needs bugs on the windshield. The dirt of the flight will prove something, I think, though I am not exactly sure what.

Flock of geese off to the right ahead, just at my altitude. This is not what I want to see! One birdstrike, and Two Nine Bravo could become a falling brick. The geese, filled with good sense, turn away.

Okay, I just checked again, and it's official. I have to turn my head *and* my shoulder to see that truck on the highway. Pedal pedal pedal, I think. Yawn. Nothing on the radio at all.

This is not an endurance record. Four hours, give or take a few minutes, is nothing. It might *feel* like an endurance test, each thermal rocking the wings, each sports car that passes that truck passing me a moment later, but in the sky the long flights are a special elite.

The longest commercial flight was run by Singapore Airlines. In an Airbus A340-500, Singapore to Newark in eighteen and a half hours.

A Boeing 777 once flew from Hong Kong to London— 11,664 nautical miles—nonstop and without refueling. Twenty-two hours and forty-two minutes. Two crews. Half the circumnavigation of the globe.

Military jets, with their refueling partners, can begin a sortie on one continent and strike in another. On a smaller scale, a female shorebird was once tracked flapping 7,145 miles from Alaska to New Zealand without landing on earth or water, and without stopping for food. The longest nonstop animal migration on earth.

In 1986, Dick Rutan and Jeana Yeager flew around the

world, nonstop, without refueling, in the *Rutan Voyager*, which now hangs in the Air and Space Museum at the Smithsonian. Nine days, three minutes, forty-four seconds. For this, they *did* get the Collier Trophy.

Twenty years later, on March 3, 2005, Steve Fossett landed the *Global Flyer* in Kansas to complete the first solo round-the-world unrefueled flight. Sixty-seven hours.

Outside of Jamestown, looking at how the water and small bluffs and folds of the James River cut the order of section roads, the legacy of Thomas Jefferson on the prairie, I have the radio tuned to Fargo Approach. Less than an hour away. Seventy-nine nautical miles. Almost home. A few moments ago, I watched a small plane pass underneath me, on final approach to the Jamestown airport, black and white airplane swift against the green farmland, and in a few more minutes, I thought, I should be able to see Fargo.

That truck with the red cab is still in sight. And to be honest, there is a part of me that wants to fly low over the interstate and buzz every car and truck there—but that would get me in trouble. Nope, I think. Not today. Nope. Not a chance. Nope. Wasn't me . . . I can hear other planes calling Fargo, but I cannot hear Fargo respond. I am still too far away. So I begin to tick off the sights, making a list, using them as a kind of countdown toward home.

Pretty little church outside—white, New England style, little steeple, near the town of Sandborn, very pretty set off against green fields.

Passing the Valley City airport, I see a valley.

Late in the afternoon, 47.4 nautical miles to the west of

town, I can see buildings and elevators on the horizon. That must be Casselton. The distance is right.

I can hear Fargo Approach now. Approach asks another plane if it can see the field.

The pilot answers no.

Approach gives him a heading, asks that he report field in sight.

Oh, I sigh. I wish that was me.

Then comes Tower City. I am back in Cass County!

I tune the radio to ATIS: "Fargo information Charlie, two one five three Zulu. Wind calm, visibility one zero, sky clear, temp two six, dew point one four, altimeter two niner niner niner, visual-approach runways three-six and two-seven in use. Inbound aircraft contact departure on one two zero point four. Notice to airmen personnel working on terminal ramp, advise on initial contact you have information Charlie."

At 5:20 in the afternoon, I can see, vague and small in the distance, but real and there nonetheless, the city of Fargo. I cannot see the airfield yet, but I'm nearly home.

Think "Ode to Joy."

"Fargo Approach, Cessna Five Three Two Nine Bravo is coming in from the west, thirty-three hundred feet, thirty-one miles out."

"Cessna Five Three Two Nine Bravo, Fargo Approach, squawk zero four five two. You full stop?" The controller sounds excited to hear me. They know I'm coming. They know about the record, and the speed, and Two Nine Bravo is a training airplane—they see it a dozen times each day, each time with a new student, a new awkwardness in the sky. This is a first, for Two Nine Bravo to do something cool.

"Zero four five two, and yes, full stop, please, Two Nine Bravo."

I wonder about the men and women in the control tower. Commercial jets all day. Military traffic. Then all the local planes. The Cessnas: Two Four One Two Mike, Six Zero Six Five Mike, and Six Five Four Seven One. There is the floatplane: One Two Four Five Five. The Seneca: Three Zero Five Four Kilo. The Navaho: Three Two Five Fox Juliet. And then, littlest in the fleet, Cessna Five Three Two Nine Bravo. Do the controllers develop affections? Does a plane carry a weight other than its pilot, passengers, baggage, and fuel?

"Fargo Approach," I say, "Cessna Five Three Two Nine Bravo with request."

"Cessna Five Three Two Nine Bravo, go ahead."

"Can you give the guys at the Jet Center a call and let them know I'm about twenty minutes out?"

"Wilco."

I already know there are television crews at the Jet Center, and I've promised to give them a heads-up before landing. This is, after all, a world record. This is special. This is neat. This is the kind of story that can fill the space in the news on a day when nothing else happens. Airplanes make cool video.

Then I suddenly worry. I've made arrangements for the tower to mark my landing time, but do they remember?

"Fargo Approach, Cessna Five Three Two Nine Bravo with one more request."

"Cessna Five Three Two Nine Bravo, what can I do for you?"

"Were you briefed that you need to mark my landing time today?"

"Absolutely, sir. Make it a good one."

"I hope so! I'll do my best."

"It's when the wheels touch, right?"

I'm laughing as I key the mic: "Well, wheels, I hope so!"

The controller keys his mic, and I can hear laughter. Then he releases the button.

"If anything else touches first just don't tell anyone," I say.

"Certainly not."

Another plane calls in on the approach frequency and asks to taxi. Approach tells him to contact ground control. Same mistake I made in Bismarck. An experimental plane without a transponder calls in with intentions to land at Jake's. In the short distance I can see the white tower of the Radisson Hotel. I can see the Fargodome. I can see the roads I know so well I've forgotten their names. I can see the homes of people I know.

"Cessna Five Three Two Nine Bravo, Fargo Approach. Just for clarification, you want like undue delay and not to be vectored around because you're doing this time thing?"

"That would be nice, Two Nine Bravo."

"Okay."

Another airplane is coming to the field at the same time as I am and told to turn 30 degrees away from the airport for sequencing. The pilot asks if he should slow down. Approach says to give it a few more miles to see, but then says, "November Six Zero Romeo, tell you what. Keep your speed up. Proceed direct for two-seven, and you can beat 'em in."

"All right. Who am I racing? I got two in sight."

"Six Zero Romeo, eleven to the left, going to three-six."

"Ah, we'll take 'em."

I am laughing. A race! I push the throttle in just a bit, then pull it back out. I am, after all, getting ready to land. But I don't care if the other plane is a fast, sleek twin-engine Seneca. I'm going to lose this race? I want my wheels to touch first. It will never happen. But it's what I want.

A woman's voice comes over the radio—a new approach controller. At first I don't understand what she says. "Cessna Two Nine Bravo, you have the field in sight?"

"Two Nine Bravo, say again?"

"Cessna Two Nine Bravo, you have the field in sight?"

"Indeed I do, Two Nine Bravo."

"Cessna Two Nine Bravo, roger. Contact the tower at one three three point eight. And understand you want runway three-six—is that correct?"

"Three-six would be great, yep, Two Nine Bravo. Going to tower."

I punch the new frequency into the radio.

"Fargo Tower, Cessna Five Three Two Nine Bravo coming into town for landing on three-six."

"Cessna Five Three Two Nine Bravo, tower." It's the same voice who was just on approach. "Runway three-six, clear to land. Seneca on two-mile final for landing on two-seven."

"I'll keep my eyes open, Two Nine Bravo."

Two-mile final. I'm about two miles out as well. Go, airplane, go! I think. I know he's much faster. But go, airplane! Go!

One more landing.

Hand on the throttle, another hand on the yoke.

Ten percent flaps, carb heat, speed of 90.

Throttle out a bit. Slowing down.

Speed of 80. Twenty percent flaps.

Speed of 70. Full flaps.

Think Copland again. *Fanfare for the Common Man.*

I cross the runway threshold.

Think of those trumpets, the blazing clarion call of the opening.

Almost. Almost.

I level off and wait. Patience. Don't force the landing.

I watch a runway stripe go by.

Think of the Emerson, Lake, and Palmer version of *Fanfare for the Common Man*. The urgent, driving bass line. The synthesizers. The drum work beyond human physics.

Almost.

It dawns on me that there are people watching this landing. At least two people in the control tower. At least two television crews, one of them a sister station to the one in Williston. They have already been running footage. A newspaper reporter. A newspaper photographer. My family, waiting at the Jet Center. The other pilots on the taxiways. Those guys in the Seneca, who are already parked. And I remember the controller telling me, just a few minutes ago, "Make it a good one."

Instinctively, I pull back on the yoke to begin a flare.

Too high!

I bounce the damn landing.

"What did you think of that?" I ask tower.

"That's called putting it down with authority," he says.

"God, I hope no one saw that."

At the Fargo Jet Center, the line guys are out in force. Television cameras rolling, they marshal me onto the ramp, orange batons waving me toward the appropriate spot. A red and white airplane in front of a pretty blue hangar. When the engine stops, my family comes out, and it's hugs all around. The line guys take a dozen photographs for the Fargo Jet Center. The reporters pin a microphone to my shirt and ask the usual questions. A world aviation speed record. What was it like?

It was fun, I say.

Postscript

E-mail from Art Greenfield, National Aeronautics Association:

Dear Scott:

Congratulations! Your record claimed on 18 July 2008 has been approved as a United States record as follows:

Class C, Aeroplanes
  Subclass: c-1b
  Group: I (Internal Combustion)
  Speed Over a Recognized Course
  Williston to Fargo: 77.89 mph
  7/18/2008
  Cessna 152

The record dossier has been forwarded to the Federation Aeronautique Internationale in Switzerland for approval as a World Record. You can track the progress of FAI's review of your record online at:

http://records.fai.org/claims.asp?id=c

We will hold your certificate for presentation at our Fall
Awards Ceremony on Monday, November 3, 2008, in
Arlington VA. If you prefer, we will mail the certificate to
you. Please let us know your preference.

Once again, congratulations on this record,

Art

And from the Fédération Aéronautique Internationale:

Sub-class: C-1b (Landplanes: take off weight 500 to 1000 kg)
    Group 1: internal combustion engine
    Speed over a recognised course:
    Williston ND (USA)–Fargo ND (USA): 125.3 km/h
    Date of: 18/07/2008
    Pilot: W. Scott OLSEN (USA)
    aircraft:
    Cessna 152 (1 Lycoming / Continental and Licensees
O-235, 110 hp)
    Registered 'N5329B'
    ratified on 08/09/2008 | Database ID 15102

The Long Cross-Country

Desire

Like everything good, it begins with a mystery. A wondering. A need to discover.

You find yourself listening to weather reports about places you've never been and imagining your talent in that particular air. Or you find yourself dreaming over maps, looking at the small blue circles, the shortest and most distant places that will welcome you safely out of the sky. The voice in the back of your head whispers, "I want to go there." And you nod. Someday, you think. Someday soon.

In my office, looking at the Raven Map of the whole of North America, my eyes cannot pass Lake Manicouagan, in Quebec, a lake that looks like a circular river, narrow but round, like an Escher print or a Möbius strip, with an island in the middle. It's the fifth-largest impact crater on Earth, one of the thousand places where something from heaven crashed into the soil. The island is called Rene-Levasseur. Its highest point is Mount Babel. And on the north side, outside the circle, in a place called Gagnon, an abandoned runway that could welcome a spaceship. What would it be like, I wonder, to fly that circle? Each time a little lower, each time a little faster. The evergreens and granite rushing by. Each time the smile on my face a little larger. Then the hard climb to see it all again. The Eye of Quebec, it's been called. An easy landing.

And if not there, perhaps then what is called the Northwest Angle of Minnesota, the little bit of land on the north side of the Lake of the Woods. At the end of the Revolutionary War, at the Treaty of Paris, the Americans wanted all of the Mississippi River, and a bad map said it went much farther north than it really does. So a line was drawn, and some ground on the north side of the lake became a part of what later became Minnesota. You can't get there by car without entering Canada first. But you can ride in a boat. Or you can fly. There is an airfield—the most northern one in the lower forty-eight—but it's a private strip. Turf. You have to have permission to land, unless it's winter, when the turf is buried in snow and you have to land on the ice road plowed in the lake. Of course, I have no good reason to go there. And that is the perfect reason to go. To find a corner, an edge, a border of any sort, and nudge it just a little.

Or somewhere, anywhere really, in the desert. The long, open red-brown land. Mesas and plateaus. Vistas over canyons and arroyos. The blue gleam of water in the distance. The way the ground can suddenly open below you and fall a thousand feet to some stream carving the rock. The Grand Canyon has its own sectional map, and I've always wanted to place my hand on the Great Unconformity. At the Grand Canyon West field, the earth falls away from the south end of the runway into a canyon so fast I cannot imagine any pilot immune to the question.

In truth, I do not fly to go anywhere. I fly to be flying. So when I imagine a trip, what I imagine most is long distance. Fargo to Bismarck, for example, then on to Dickinson, the Badlands of North Dakota. Then on to Miles City, Montana, then Billings and my friends at the tanker base, where they refuel and reload the airplanes that drop slurry on wildfires. Then even farther to Livingston, where in my imagination I spend a night and the next morning rise over the last bit of flatland before crossing into Paradise Valley and following the Yellowstone River south, a hard turn east through the high, hard walls of Yankee Jim Canyon, past the slick chute mountain face called the Devil's Slide, until the airplane slows and descends and finally lands in Gardiner, at the north end of Yellowstone National Park, a mountain airfield graced by a river on one side. Six hundred and nineteen point seven miles from here to there. Six hundred and nineteen point seven miles from there back home.

The solo long cross-country is a rite of passage, a part of every student pilot's training. Can you get there, wherever there might be? Can you draw a line on your chart, mark the waypoints on the ground, calculate your time and fuel and what heading you need to fly to compensate for the wind? Once you take off, and once you leave the familiar sites of your town, can you find a place to land? Every pilot does this. No shorter than 150 nautical miles. No fewer than three landings. And when every pilot lands and ties down the airplane, what they have is a new story. An adventure. A success. And once you have the full ticket in your hand, once you are no longer a student but a real pilot, you begin to dream the larger dreams. Where can I go? you wonder. Every place I see on the map has a call for me, an urging to come visit. But there has always been one place to go first. My father was a private pilot, though he hasn't flown in probably forty-five years. My mother was a flight attendant for Trans World Airlines. Because I made the mistake of being reasonable, I did not learn to fly when I was young. But now, more than anything else, I want to land an airplane and see them smile. I want to bring an airplane home.

Fargo to Jackson, Minnesota. Jackson to Creston, Iowa. Creston to Camdenton, Missouri. Five hundred and sixty-nine point five miles from home to home. Five hundred and sixty-nine point five miles back. One day down and one day back, when the hard cold and storms of a prairie winter break and I can get into the air.

Departure

The ATIS today has a woman's voice: "Fargo information Papa, one three five three Zulu. Wind one seven zero at one one. Visibility one zero. Sky clear, temperature minus two two. Dew point minus two four. Altimeter three zero four four. Visual-approach runway one-eight in use. Inbound aircraft contact approach on one two zero point four. Notice to airmen, runway niner PAPI out of service. Advise on initial contact you have Papa."

The voice in my headset, automated, repeats itself while I organize the cockpit. Charts on one clipboard, flight plans on another. A small suitcase and the airplane engine's thermal blanket stuffed behind my seat. A silver travel mug of fresh hot coffee, for now, on the dash. The preflight check

THE LONG CROSS-COUNTRY

of the airplane is done. The fuel is topped off, and I have extra oil on board. I go through the checklist and everything looks good, every item in place. The only thing left is for me to turn the key and get this thing in the air.

"Okay," I say to myself. Then I key the microphone. "Fargo Ground, Cessna Five Three Two Nine Bravo is at the north ramp, ready to go. Departing to the southeast, at or below three thousand. Information Papa."

A woman's polite voice comes back. "Cessna Two Nine Bravo, did you say you were at the south ramp?"

"Nope, north ramp, please, Two Nine Bravo."

"Cessna Five Three Two Nine Bravo, Fargo Ground. Taxi to runway one-eight at Charlie via Charlie. Maintain three thousand. Departure frequency one two zero point four. Squawk zero four zero seven."

"Going to one-eight at Charlie via Charlie. I'll stay below three thousand. Squawk zero four zero seven, Two Nine Bravo."

"Cessna Two Nine Bravo, verify you have information Papa."

"Information Papa, yes, Two Nine Bravo."

"Roger and a new weather will be coming out here shortly. Wind one five zero at one two, altimeter three zero four three."

"Three zero four three, thank you."

A final look around. A last sip before the coffee goes into a little pocket behind the right seat. Then the throttle goes in. "And away we go," I say to no one except myself. Two Nine Bravo taxis to runway one-eight. I go through the final checks and then the run-up. The engine sounds strong and even.

"I don't think there's anything else I need to do," I say to myself. "Fuel looks good. Pressure looks good. Temperature looks good. Everything looks good."

"Fargo Tower," I say, "Cessna Five Three Two Nine Bravo is at runway one-eight at Charlie, ready to go."

"Cessna Five Three Two Nine Bravo, Fargo Tower, runway one-eight at Charlie, fly runway heading, cleared for takeoff."

"Runway heading, cleared for takeoff, Two Nine Bravo. Thank you."

The throttle goes in. The little airplane begins to roll. Feet first for steering, then the firming up of the yoke. Eyes on the runway and eyes on the airspeed indicator. At sixty, a little back pressure. Suddenly and gracefully we are in the sky. A little rudder to keep straight. A huge smile on my face. I am rising over what looks like an ocean of snow, frozen waves receding to every horizon. The reflected sunlight is brilliant and hard.

"Cessna Two Nine Bravo, turn left on course and contact departure. G'day."

"Going to departure, Two Nine Bravo. Thank you."

I press the button to change radio frequencies, then key the microphone.

"Fargo Departure, Cessna Five Three Two Nine Bravo is just past the airport, coming up on two thousand feet, departing to the southeast."

"Cessna Five Three Two Nine Bravo, Fargo Departure, radar contact." There is a slowing, a hesitation in his voice. "You're departing to the southeast, departing the area? You're not going to the practice area?"

Two Nine Bravo is an old airplane. It's a slow airplane,

too. It's been a trainer here for most of its life. The men and women in the tower have watched it day after day go to a practice area and then return. Students and instructors learning how to recover from a stall, how to do ground reference maneuvers, how to side slip and forward slip and do climbing turns and descending turns. Students and instructors going through the curriculum that teaches someone how to fly. But rarely anything more.

"Nope. Going down to Missouri. Two Nine Bravo."

"Cessna Two Nine Bravo, roger," he says. His voice sounds surprised, and almost proud of this little plane. "Proceed on course. Maintain three thousand."

"Three thousand, will do. Two Nine Bravo."

It is nine o'clock in the morning.

At three thousand feet I level off, reduce power, lean the fuel mixture just a bit. I watch cars on the interstate and cars in the neighborhoods, too. When the town falls away behind me, I scan the horizons as often as the instruments, the land below and the land far away. Part of me picks out the possible emergency landing sites if a problem appears. Part of me dreams a story of history and imagination. After a short while, Fargo Departure comes back on the air.

"Cessna Two Nine Bravo, radar service terminated. Squawk one two zero zero, frequency change approved. Have a good flight."

"Thank you very much. Going VFR, Two Nine Bravo."

I am gone!

Winter
There are clouds to the west.

Not the bright drama of summer thunderstorms. No immense churning of heat and water into wind and terror. Not the flash of lightning or the gut-tightening grays of a gust front. Just a thickening of the sky. The God blue of outer space becoming the dirty blue of wind and cold and soil and snow. Snow.

I am glad I'm not flying that direction.

The temperature when I left home this morning was 10 degrees below o Fahrenheit. When I started the airplane, the ATIS said it was minus 22 Celsius, which is minus 8 Fahrenheit. Either way, it's a cold morning. But it's also clear and bright. Sun dogs rise with the sun, three stars in the morning sky. And the snowfields below me shimmer like water.

On the telephone earlier this morning, with the man from Flight Service who gave me the weather briefing, he paused after reading the temperature and said, "I bet you're going to get some good performance out of that airplane today!" I laughed and assured him I would.

Cold air is dense air. Dense air means more air moving over the wings, which means a faster climb rate, a shorter takeoff roll, an easier bird to keep in the sky. But cold also means ice. "Multiple icing levels," the briefer told me. Oh, great, I thought. I don't fly in clouds, so the icing should not be a problem, but still—there it was in front of me. Ice in the air. Supercooled water looking for something to grab onto. The wings, the tail, the landing gear, the radio antennae. All of it can collect the ice that makes the airplane heavy, that makes the airplane slow, that makes the wings the wrong shape for lift, that makes the airplane fall out of the sky. There is no such thing as clear-air icing, so I should be fine. But if I have to fly under clouds, and if there is a rain falling from those clouds, and if that rain is a freezing rain, then I will be flying some other direction.

Winter is hard on the prairie. The record cold for Fargo and Moorhead is minus 48 degrees Fahrenheit, even though this number is a bit suspicious. On the phone one day with my friend Daryl Ritchison, a meteorologist, he says, "In 1887 there was no standard for measuring temperature. That record was recorded with an open-air thermometer. It was, in effect, measuring the temperature of the thermometer instead of the air—lots of radiant heating and cooling with those. Still, that's pretty cold."

Coldest windchill in town: minus 90 on the old chart, minus 60 to 70 on the new scale. Fastest temperature drop: 50 degrees in twenty-four hours, though we got pretty close to that in just nine hours two years ago. And we knew it was coming. Days in advance, the storm was forming in Canada, and on television Daryl was sounding the alarm. We watched the front move down the front range of the Canadian Rockies and spread east over the plains. Students went to lunch in shorts, to dinner in survival suits.

"Keep in mind," Daryl says, "our big storms are mostly re-formations. Something big comes in off the Pacific, and it gets ripped to shreds by the Rockies. We're still pretty much in the rain shadow of the mountains here—most of our moisture comes from the Gulf of Mexico. Most of the Midwest would be nearly desert if the Gulf didn't act the way it does. Anyway, if the Pacific storms cross over Colorado or Alberta, that's where the mountains are the highest, then they get slowed down, but that wave of energy is still there and they have the time to pull themselves back together. If the storms cross somewhere else, say, Wyoming or Montana, they get torn apart but they don't get slowed down, so they don't have the time to re-form before they get to us. But if you get a good strong wave crossing in Colorado, and lots of moisture coming up from the Gulf, then it's going to be a real event."

There are clouds to the west, and I watch them all morning. "Winter is very, very subtle," Daryl tells me. I remember this as, looking at the ground, the way lines of trees sometimes form complete circles, it dawns on me that I'm looking at lakes. They are not very big, frozen and snow covered, but almost by surprise I see how the trees define the shape of the shore. I start counting. One, two, three, four, five, six, seven—at least seven lakes nearly invisible under the snow. Subtle as well as hard. "And Arctic or polar air is very shallow," he continues. "Cold air sinks." There is a weak stationary front over the James River in North Dakota this morning, and the wind is out of the southeast. It has to rise ever so little when it meets the front, and the rising air creates the clouds. Very low clouds. The kind I can't fly under. The kind that make a landing field invisible.

Those clouds are not chasing me. I am not running from weather this morning. But I can see them as clearly as I can see the weathered farmstead passing below me and the frozen river winding into the southern distance. There's nobody out there. No cars on the section roads, no motion on the farms of any kind.

The briefer warned me of multiple icing levels. And so I will watch those clouds, just wondering, all morning.

Art

On the ground, there is no way to imagine the world is this pretty. Sure, there are photographs from airplanes and from outer space. We've seen the mountain flybys in the movies and the rush of water toward some beachfront on television. We have calendars in our offices and homes that show us what the pilot, the astronaut, the skydiver sees. But each of these is static and cold. It's one thing to see the ceiling of the Sistine Chapel in a book, worried that your coffee might spill, listening to the radio or to children or traffic, and it's quite another thing to be standing, looking up at the thing itself, feeling your soul rise toward that promise. Art is not only representation. Art is experience. Your gut has to be there as well as your eyes or your ears. There is a feeling to art, a way the insides of your knees can know Mozart or Le Cordon Bleu, the way your shoulders can know a poem.

Three thousand feet above sea level, two thousand feet above this bit of ground, what I see this morning is how every little farmstead rests just off center on the border of the section of land. Every section a square. Every section carved out of the ice and snow like the sheets of a wedding cake, surrounded by the browns of country roads. Shelterbelts look like a Charles Beck print.

When I pass a small tree farm, young evergreens surrounded by a shelterbelt of much older oaks and maples, Beautiful country, I say to myself. I pass a small lonely-looking weathered barn sitting unprotected in the middle of a frozen and ice-covered section of land. That would not have been fun, I think. Whatever home would have been next to it is gone.

I am sure there are stories. You look at these farms, the falling-down and abandoned and gray barns and houses and shacks, the tracks on the land, the trees sticking out of the snow in some unlikely spot, like the single tree in the frozen lake at the lowest circle of hell. You look at the curve of a frozen stream running through a field, and there is no way not to wonder what the first people here thought of winter. Blizzards and sun dogs. Hard, hard cold.

The ground passes beneath me, section after section of land go by, and I remember Daryl telling me that winter is subtle. Twenty thousand shades of white and gray, I think. Twenty thousand just to begin to talk about how sunlight reflects off farmland snowfields, and how that reflection changes with the angle of the sun rising into the sky, the sun dogs diminishing. And how to describe, how to include, the hint of very cold air I get on my face and hands, despite the cabin heat being turned on full? How do I include the sound of the engine, the radio calls, the small lifts and bumps of the air? How do I say the way my finger rests on the trim wheel is a part of the beauty of this land? There are horses at the farmstead to my right. There is a field of corn standing off to my left.

First the Red River, and then the Buffalo River, and now just the small streams—they all are frozen. You wouldn't even know they are there. But the trees that border them make a line, curving and twisting, a line that contradicts and perhaps betrays the order of the section roads.

Coming up on a little wetland here, some ponds and some reeds, the color of the earth changes from the shock of white snow to the mottled brown of plants and water. Even though this is ice today, you can tell that this is habitat, wetland, a place where water pools.

The town of Morris goes by. The town of Montevideo goes by. On the radio, I listen to airplanes self-announce their arrivals and departures. There's a helicopter landing in Milbank, and I have to look at my chart because I didn't think South Dakota was so close, but it is.

I cannot explain the beauty of shelterbelts and section roads. Just squares cut into the snowcap of a prairie winter. But then it hits me. It's like looking at a painting by Piet Mondrian. The white canvas, the straight black lines, the boxes of color. Hard black lines. Primary colors. The red box here. The blue box there. The yellow box too. The right angles and high contrast. "The absolute harmony of straight lines and pure colors underlying the visible world," he said. Neoplasticism replacing cubism. Eleven paintings completely redone after he fled Europe and World War II, to give them more "boogie-woogie."

Off to the right I can see Big Stone Lake and the Traverse Gap. This, I think, is the place where everything changes, although you can't see it from the ground. This was the southern end of Lake Agassiz, the continent's largest inland sea ever, at its best in the Pleistocene. There are shark teeth in the bedrock here. Water on the north side of the gap flows to Hudson Bay and then into the Arctic. Water on the south side flows to the Gulf of Mexico. A continental divide on the prairie. The water on the north side becomes the Red River of the North, which flows past my home. The water on the south side becomes the Minnesota River, which flows into the Mississippi. Once upon a real time, the books say the drainage was sudden, catastrophic, gouging a valley to the south that the river would never fill. Glacial River Warren, long since gone, was one of the three main drains for the retreating lake. Today, though, the lake is long and narrow. Small islands named Goose and Manhattan and Skeleton and Mud and Kite and Pancake and Frying Pan. Cottonwoods, ash, silver maple trees define the frozen shoreline.

Two Nine Bravo flies along, and I am wondering what

Thomas Jefferson, the great surveyor, the president who commanded that the country be measured and marked, the man responsible for the unfailing lines that have become the midwestern section roads, would think about redoing it all for more boogie-woogie. Then—and who knows why these thoughts come when they do—I get another image: the frozen sections and weathered gray farmsteads look exactly like the old World War II photographs, taken by pilots in airplanes, of convoys of ships at sea.

First Stop: Jackson, Minnesota
I have been wanting to play all morning.

Flying over the town of Herman, the one small runway next to the roadway on the northwest side of town, I wanted to swoop down and do a touch-and-go, for no good reason at all other than I wanted to swoop. I'm not sure I've ever swooped before, and it sounded like a good thing to do. I didn't, though. The notion of swooping occurred too late.

Then somewhere south of Montevideo, I looked at my GPS and discovered I'd been creeping to the east. I had to get back on course. I could have turned gently; I wasn't that far away from the direct line. But turning gently isn't any fun, so I put the plane in a steep turn to the right and pulled back on the yoke to hold the altitude. I smiled when I felt the minor g-force push me more firmly into the seat. Of course, this steep turn was an overcorrection. So I had to do another one to the left. Then another one to the right. S turns over the southern Minnesota farmland. A normal person on the ground would have thought I was nuts. A pilot on the ground would have smiled.

When I get close to Jackson, however, I have to get to

business. The headwind I've been pressing into is really a crosswind here. Crosswind landings take a bit of skill. The runway is pointed toward 130 degrees, and the last check I heard put the wind at 170 degrees. Forty degrees of crosswind and blowing hard.

Ten miles out, I start looking for the airport. The charts tell me it's on the north side of town. I have the diagram from the airport directory, and I have an aerial picture from the Internet just for good measure, but the picture was taken in summertime. I do not see the runway. All I see now is the white of snowfields and the dark lines of roads.

Six miles out I'm self-announcing on the radio, and the GPS says I'm on track. And when I see the airport, the one runway set into the snow (the second runway, turf, is buried), it looks very small.

This runway is 75 feet wide and 3,591 feet long. The main runway back home is 150 feet wide and 9,000 feet long. The shortest Fargo runway is 3,800 feet long and still 150 feet wide. This, I think, is going to be fun.

I line up with the runway and bank the wings to the right to correct for the crosswind. To keep from turning, though, I have to push the rudder to the left. I put the runway numbers on top of the engine cowling and reduce power. Ninety knots. Reduce power. Eighty knots. Reduce power. Start with the flaps. Seventy knots. I bank harder to keep straight with the wind. I push more rudder to keep straight toward the centerline. One hand on the yoke. One hand on the throttle. I smile at the memory of the first time I did this, how completely weird it was to come in for a landing tilted hard to one side. My left foot has the rudder pedal pressed completely to the floor. If I don't like it, I can always go around. But I like this one. I like this one a lot.

Just past the runway threshold, I am low enough to level out, to straighten out, to flare and then touch down. Not even a wobble.

I pull up to the fuel pump and shut down the airplane. Getting out, I stretch and flex. This is self-service, so I walk around and grab the grounding wire. This prevents sparks, which is a very good thing to prevent around fuel. I attach it to the exhaust, then begin to walk toward the fuel pump. A sharp click and a whine make me turn around. The grounding wire has retracted and is snugly back on its spool. I pull it out again and attach it again. I pause. Nothing. I turn toward the fuel. The click and whine.

The airport manager, or someone who acts like one, comes out smiling. "Flight Service just called for you," he says.

"What?" I ask, amazed.

"Yeah, you're late," he says. "They wanted to know if you were on the ground yet, and I told them you were just pulling up."

I didn't think I'd fallen that far behind.

Looking at the grounding wire, the manager smiles again. "You have to pull this one all the way out," he says.

I fuel Two Nine Bravo and then go inside. It's a nice little terminal. But there's no coffee. I call Flight Service to officially close the first flight plan and learn that the headwinds are stronger than predicted. I'm going to have trouble making it all the way before darkness sets in.

Back in the airplane, I taxi to the beginning of runway one-three and give it the gas.

Why I Love Three Thousand Feet

I remember a winter's night a great many years ago. I was lucky enough to be in a private jet, flying from somewhere east to somewhere west, and we had just passed forty thousand feet. I knelt in the small space between and behind the crew. The pilot showed me the lights of St. Louis and the lights of Chicago at the same time. I could see the curve of the earth. It was all very pretty and all very quiet. Disconnected, too. I remember thinking that we had somehow moved from the world of body and blood to the world of math.

In every pilot's flight bag there is a book called *The FAR/ AIM*. It comes out every year. *The Federal Aviation Regulations/Aeronautical Information Manual*. It's the rule book for flying. It's a fat book, government- and legalspeak, and also the voice of experience. You think you're alone in the sky, for example, because airplanes, even very big airplanes, are hard to see unless there is some high-contrast background—or if they are very close. Even an airplane at your altitude and flying directly at you remains a pinprick in the sky until you're screaming and pushing the yoke hard down and hoping to God that there's time and enough space in the air.

So there are rules to keep the airplanes apart. And some of those rules say how high.

91.159 VFR cruising altitude or flight level.

> Except while holding in a holding pattern of 2 minutes or less, or while turning, each person operating an aircraft under VFR in level cruising flight more than 3,000 feet above the surface shall maintain the appropriate altitude or flight level prescribed below, unless otherwise authorized by ATC:

(a)   When operating below 18,000 feet MSL and—
    (1)   On a magnetic course of zero degrees through 179 degrees, any odd thousand foot MSL altitude +500 feet (such as 3,500, 5,500, or 7,500); or
    (2)   On a magnetic course of 180 degrees through 359 degrees, any even thousand foot MSL altitude +500 feet (such as 4,500, 6,500, or 8,500).
(b)   When operating above 18,000 feet MSL, maintain the altitude or flight level assigned by ATC.

But notice the exception: "more than 3000 feet above the surface." Of course, below three thousand feet there are rules as well.

91.119 Minimum safe altitudes: General
Except when necessary for takeoff and landing, no person may operate an aircraft below the following altitudes:
(a)   Anywhere. An altitude allowing, if a power unit fails, an emergency landing without undue hazard to persons or property on the surface.
(b)   Over congested areas: Over any congested area of a city, town, or settlement, or over any open air assembly of persons, an altitude of 1,000 feet above the highest obstacle within a horizontal radius of 2,000 feet of the aircraft.
(c)   Over other than congested areas: An altitude of 500 feet above the surface, except over open water or sparsely populated areas. In those cases, the aircraft may not be operated closer than 500 feet to any person, vessel, vehicle, or structure.

Passing from southern Minnesota into Iowa, my airspeed is 93 knots, 2,200 rpm. My ground speed is only 73.5 knots. The altimeter in Two Nine Bravo says three thousand feet. But that would be true only if I were flying over the ocean on what is called a standard day. The prairie beneath me is roughly twelve hundred feet above sea level, so my real altitude is eighteen hundred feet. At this altitude, I can tell you the color of your mittens. I can even tell you if they match. I can tell you if the car is rusted and if the window is open. At eighteen hundred feet I get everything. Distance and intimacy. The clouds that won't be here for hours. Snow angels in the farmstead's backyard.

A short distance away from Jackson, south of a town called Pocahontas and east of a town called Storm Lake, a wind farm passes below me. Far too many to count, the white piers and elegant blades turn slowly. It has all the order of a well-planned English garden. In the midst of the wind farm, however, there are farmsteads. Yellow outbuildings. Quonset huts. Shelterbelts. The weathered gray hulk, listing heavily to starboard, of a very old barn.

I wonder, as I pass over the blades, what it must be like to live here. Humbling, each daybreak, to see the rotation of the earth brought down to those towers and turned into power? Or something larger, more encouraging, each spin of the blades sending off into infinity a type of hope, like a Tibetan prayer flag, each snap sending a prayer to heaven?

"Infinity for the human eye is thirty-six inches."

I am on the telephone with Dr. Gary Renier, an optometrist in Fargo and a fine photographer. I am asking about the way a person sees distance, about how the human eye, the pilot's eye, can scan an instrument panel and then the ground. And I am wondering if there is distance where the distance no longer matters, like the infinity setting on a camera lens.

"That's all?" I ask.

"That's it," he says. "But you need to remember there's a lot of other things going on that affect your sight from the airplane."

He runs me through the familiar stuff about the rods and cones in the back of the eye—cones pick up color, rods pick up black and white; cones are more sensitive, rods are more peripheral—but then we start to talk about limits. "Even if your vision is 20/20 in the macular," he says, "that's only in one part of your eye. And that good part can be only two degrees of the eye. Your vision in the periphery can be 20/100. So you have to scan. We all scan, all the time.

"And especially now, with the snow, we have to filter the monochromatic landscape to see the waves of snow, the way a snow skier would use an amber lens. At two thousand feet above the ground you can still pick up colors. At higher altitude, there is a lot less oxygen and lots more ultraviolet radiation between you and ground. Both of these make what you're seeing more difficult. And there's a lot more UV coming off the North Dakota snow than there is off, say, the Texas desert."

"What about the UV filter for a camera lens?" I ask. "What about the UV rating on my sunglasses and in the windshield of the airplane?"

"They're great, aren't they?" he asks. "But remember that they are filters. They are removing wavelengths from what you see. If you had polarized gray lenses in your glasses, you would have a very hard time seeing a green light on your dash. The wavelengths are too close. Ever notice that a stop sign isn't really red? It has a little bit of orange in it. And ever notice that green lights are sort of a lime green with a little yellow in them? Those are both because of how we see, and how we age. Men especially have a color deficit as they get older."

"What about just the brightness of the snow?"

"There's a trade-off," he says. "The smaller the pupil, the better your depth perception, the better your depth of field."

Pilots talk about five types of altitude: Indicated Altitude is what the altimeter says when it's set to the current air pressure. True Altitude is the distance above sea level. Absolute Altitude is the distance above the ground. Pressure Altitude is what the altimeter would say if the pressure scale were set to 29.92, a theoretical standard. Density Altitude is the pressure altitude corrected for temperature.

Each type of altitude has its purpose. Indicated Altitude is a way to say where you are compared to other airplanes. Absolute Altitude is a number to keep you alive. Density Altitude tells you how the airplane will behave. But perhaps there should be a sixth type of altitude. The altitude of appreciation, perhaps. Or the altitude of participation. Between the Rockies and the Appalachians, between the Gulf of Mexico and the Beaufort Sea, three thousand feet means you can see the people outside the house, standing next to a car, at a farmstead underneath a wind tower, and when two of them wave at you, and you rock your wings in reply, you can see the other two wave as well.

Crashing in Iowa

The snow on the ground is going away. Every mile south there seems to be just a little less. It's a bit like watching a movie with the seasons set to fast-forward. South of Jackson, crossing the Iowa border, the snow looks more like splats of white paint thrown against the brown earth. Wind splats, I think. I can tell the direction of the wind in the storm that made these marks. It was from the northwest. And where there is no snow I can see the marks left by tractors and plows in the earth. They seem to be the same in every field. But then I realize that every mark is an individual history. A mark made by one farmer driving one tractor with one hope in mind, that the earth would remember this mark and turn into something good.

Every single one of them wanted to get here fast. The schedule was full and hard, and speed was important. The bus wasn't working. But a plane was nearby, a Beechcraft Bonanza. And there was a pilot who was willing. They checked the weather more than once. There was bad weather coming. But they felt they could get under it and speed along just fine. Some of the guys on the bus flipped a coin to see who would go.

On February 3, 1959, Buddy Holly, Ritchie Valens, and Jiles Richardson—the Big Bopper—died in an Iowa plane crash. They took off late from Mason City, just after one in the morning, in light snow, and crashed almost immediately, about five miles north of the airport. Witnesses say they could see the red taillight go down. The reports say the pilot was in a plane he didn't really know, in weather conditions he did not anticipate, with a different type of altitude indicator or artificial horizon than he was familiar with. The instrument in the Bonanza would read exactly the opposite of what he was used to. He was a commercial pilot but not an instrument pilot. In fact, he had failed an instrument-check ride. Weather briefers did not tell him about the incoming weather because he did not ask.

Only the pilot's body was found inside the airplane. The others had been hurled away by the force of the crash. Holly was twenty-two years old. Richardson was twenty-eight. Valens was seventeen. The pilot, Roger Peterson, was only twenty-one. They were on their way to Moorhead, landing at Hector Field in Fargo.

Leaving Jackson, Mason City is only minutes to the east.

And then there was the other crash everyone knows. United Airlines Flight 232 from Denver to Chicago. July 19, 1989. A DC-10. Two hundred and eighty-five passengers; 11 crew members. A perfectly normal flight in clear daylight weather. Little packages of peanuts. A choice of soda or coffee. Wine in first class. But then a fan disk in the engine in the tail came apart, exploded really, and shrapnel cut through all three hydraulic systems. The pilot, a man named Alfred Haynes, had no flight controls. No elevators. No rudder. No ailerons. Nothing to steer or control the airplane. First officer William Records and flight engineer Dudley Dvorak knew this was not going to end well. In the back, a DC-10 instructor also knew the play had gone off-script. He offered to help, and when he got up front he learned all they had were the engines under the wings. Power the right one a bit more, and they could turn to the left. Power the left one for a turn to the right. Reduce power on both, and they could descend. So he kneeled on the cockpit floor and put both hands on the thrust controls.

Later investigations would discover the fan had a crack, and the crack should have been seen during inspections, and the crack was due to a problem with the way the blade was made. But for now all that mattered was getting the plane to the ground. At Sioux City, they rolled the fire trucks and alerted the hospitals. The plane dumped fuel and turned to reduce altitude, then tried to line up with the shorter runway, where the fire trucks were waiting, having been told the long runway would be used. Everyone scrambled.

They almost made it. Going too fast, descending too quickly, they almost made it. But a wing clipped the ground, the airplane broke apart, everything caught on fire, and all hell came to visit. One hundred and eleven people died. One hundred and eighty-five people survived, though 111 of those were injured.

Leaving Jackson, Sioux City is only minutes to the west.

Pilots carry crash stories. When the machine breaks, your heart breaks with it, imagining the fight on the way down, the checklists and the imagination trying to find a way to avoid gravity. When the pilot makes a bad decision, though, you feel something different. You feel bad for the people in back, and for their families, but you shake your head at the pilot. Flying does not forgive the unprepared or the foolish. It's a shame, you think. He should have known better. We imagine ourselves in the left seat, and add that story to the list of what not to do.

Some things you do in the back of your head. You do them always, but not with any real effort. It's a part of the training. Make something so common, so usual, so part of the routine that you fail to notice anymore that it's what you're doing. Picking out emergency landing places is one of these for a pilot. And for a pilot like me, midwestern, flatland, rural, mostly daytime flying, it's easy. Section roads are the best. A level field could do. The interstate highways would provide some interesting stories back home. If the machine breaks, there is a very large difference between an emergency landing and a crash.

Central Iowa, the snow giving way to brown earth, though the lakes are still frozen, and Two Nine Bravo is humming along. The headwind remains, but otherwise this is a perfect flight. No bad weather. No turbulence. No problems with the navigation or the machine. But I still see a road and think, "I could land there." Then I forget it. A few minutes later, I think, "I could land there." And then I forget it.

The headwind remains. My airspeed is 90 knots. My ground speed is 67.5. That's a little more than 75 miles an hour, the speed limit on I-29 in the Dakotas. This is going to be a long flight.

Still an hour north of Creston, I pick out an emergency landing site but then wonder about my choice. What I see looks like a serpent, an old-school etching of a sea monster. No, I think, it's Nessie! The Loch Ness Monster. Black humps rising out of a white sea. When I get a bit closer, I see it's a country road cutting across a small bundle of hills, though *hill* is too strong of a word. Rises? Wrinkles? Something like that. When the road crests each small elevation, the wind has scraped the snow and ice away and left it brown. In each depression, the snow remains.

"Can't land there," I think. And then I start laughing,

because I can imagine trying. Each rise throwing me and Two Nine Bravo back into the air like a Motocross racer on a motorcycle. Or, to be more exact, me and Two Nine Bravo riding the hills like that Claymation figure riding the hills on an electric razor in the old Christmas-special television commercials.

Getting out of trouble is serious business. Imagining trouble, even when your imagination is a bit off center, is one way to never get there in the first place.

Good-bye T-Rex

I admit I am looking for a crash site, another mark on the earth. Even from three thousand feet I should be able to see it. It should be huge. I know it's invisible from the ground now, but my hope says there should be something, some echo, some mark only those people looking for it will be able to see from altitude. This is something important. This is something I want to see.

In the history of crashes, this is one of the big ones, though very few people know about it. A gigantic earth-cracking, sky-blackening, thunder-whomping crash. Straight out of the heavens. Literally. And it's been all swept away, covered up, hidden from anyone without the expertise and the special equipment you need to see it.

Imagine a lush, subtropical sea. Imagine an earth much warmer than now. It's seventy-four million years ago, give or take a few. Iowa doesn't look much like Iowa. It has a coastline. In the water there are Mosasaurs, Pterosaurs, and Plesiosaurs (Nessie!). On the ground there are Hadrosaurs, Alamosaurus, Torosaurus, Paprasaurolophus, Troodons and Triceratops, Tyrannosaurus.

It's a typical day, whatever a typical day may have been

like, and then a whoosh before the wham. And then everything is gone. A stony meteorite two kilometers across falls
out of the sky, and the resulting crater is twenty-five miles
across. Everything in Iowa is dead. So is everything in Nebraska, Missouri, Illinois, Wisconsin, and Minnesota. The
early research on this site proposed that this was the hit
that took out everything—all the dinosaurs, nearly everything on earth. No one knew this crater was here until core
samples from wells revealed a pattern. But the big one, the
hit that took out everything, the K-T Boundary Extinction
Event, happened sixty-five million years ago. Manson, they
discovered, was just the warm-up act. It's ten million years
older, give or take a few.

So, I think, blast a chunk out of Iowa, and I should be
able to see it. I should be able to see some part of it. Some
hill. Some ridge. Some something! This is the largest crater
in the United States. But I already know why I cannot. The
glaciers came. The ice sheets and the grinding cold. The land
was scraped. The crater was filled in. And when the glaciers
retreated, the land was smoothed and leveled. According to
the surveys, there are between seventy and three hundred
feet of glacial till on top of the hole.

Flying along, I pass just west of Manson and certainly
over some part of the crater. All I can see are flatland sections, farmsteads, country roads. Cows where there used to
be dinosaurs.

Multiple windmills.

Second Stop: Creston, Iowa
If I had time, I think, I would turn. Thirty miles northwest
of Creston, I know I could turn east. It wouldn't take very

much time. A few minutes more, and I could be over Madison County, Iowa. I've never read the book, and I have not seen the movie, but I do know about the covered bridges there. And hunting for bridges from the air, following the tree-marked riverbanks until they come into view, seems like a wonderful way to spend some time in the sky. The snow is mostly gone, and the air is much warmer. I could even open the window. But time is something I no longer have today.

Another narrow runway. Another short runway, too, though this one is longer than Jackson. Another crosswind test. Another solid landing.

As I pull up to the terminal building, however, there is a problem. There is a jet parked in front of the fuel tanks. Parked. Locked and silent. I sit there for a moment just looking at it, engine running. Now what do I do? I know I can get out my chart and directory and look for the closest airport that sells aviation gas. I have enough gas in Two Nine Bravo to fly for another hour or more. But I want gas here. Gas here gives me enough to make it the final leg.

A man comes out of the terminal and walks toward me and Two Nine Bravo. I shut down the airplane.

"Can I get gas?" I ask when he's close, pointing at the jet.

"Oh, sure," he says. "Go on inside. Leave it all to me."

I roll myself out of the airplane, grab my cold coffee mug, and go inside. The man grabs Two Nine Bravo near the hub of the propeller and pulls her close to the jet. He attaches the ground wire and uncoils the fuel line. Good, I think. Very good.

Inside, the coffee is strong and hot. I call Flight Service to close this leg and ask about the next, and the briefer tells me that if I climb to five thousand feet I can get out of the headwind.

I don't like five thousand feet, but I tell him that's where I'll be. Five thousand five hundred, to be exact.

I pay for the gas and climb back in the airplane. One more leg, I say to myself. Almost there.

Which way is three-one and which way is one-three?

Many small airports use the same radio frequency. All day, you can hear pilots announce their takeoffs and landings, their turns and altitudes, and check where they are against where you are. You can announce your own position if you need to, just so they know you are there. The language is scripted, concise, exact, and unambiguous. But sometimes the conversations get a little strange. I won't say where, but on the radio I hear a conversation between two pilots, both arriving at the same small airport at the same time. I don't think I'll give their tail numbers, either.

PILOT 1: Five miles out, entering downwind for left traffic, runway one-three.
PILOT 2: Six miles out, entering downwind for left traffic, runway one-three.

A short while later:

PILOT 1: Downwind for left traffic, runway one-three.

A pause.

PILOT 2: Which runway are you using?
PILOT 1: One-three.
PILOT 2: Sure looks like you're using three-one to me.
PILOT 1: No, one-three.

Silence.

PILOT 2: Which way are you pointed, northeast or southwest?

PILOT 1: I am flying a heading of three one, I am about to turn to base and then one-three.

PILOT 2: Look, I can see you, and you are not . . .

PILOT 1: On final to runway one-three.

PILOT 2: What numbers do you see on the runway?

PILOT 1: A one and a three.

PILOT 2: Yeah, but which one is first? Come on, I can see . . .

Silence.

PILOT 2: I'm sorry. What I was looking at isn't even an airplane.

PILOT 1: On the ground, runway one-three.

Final Approach

There is no snow in Missouri. The rivers have ice in the slow spots, and some farm ponds have a thin covering, too, but the earth is brown and black and open. When I cross the winding and chocolate-colored Missouri River, I smile. Even though I have not lived here for a very long time, this is home ground. I was born in Kansas City. I went to college and the first bit of graduate school in Columbia. This is the state where I fell in love. This is where I got married. This is where I got a great many speeding tickets. This is where my parents and my sister live. This is where my wife's sister and my father's sister live. I have friends, good friends, on both sides of the state as well as in the middle. This is where people know the old stories. Nearly every road has seen my tires. But this is the first time I've come in from the sky.

When I cross the Missouri, my GPS tells me there is military airspace in front of me. Whiteman Air Force Base is ahead and off to the west. Home of the B2 bomber. I wonder what they must think of little planes like Two Nine Bravo. Every single pilot there began his or her training in a plane like this one. Every single pilot there, though, has moved on. Someone there is watching me on a radar screen. We will not talk to each other. But that person will watch.

I cross I-70. I pass Sedalia, too. Every sight is familiar, though from altitude they come to me as fresh and wonder giving as if they were new.

When the lake shows up, the long Gravois arm of the Lake of the Ozarks, I feel like I could coast in on the memories alone. Farmland gives way to forest first. And the gunmetal gray of winter water in twilight.

Landing

"Camdenton, Cessna Five Three Two Nine Bravo. Ten miles out. Coming straight in for runway one-five, Camdenton."

I do not expect an answer, but suddenly there is one.

"Cessna Two Nine Bravo, Camdenton. Winds one seventy at ten."

I look for the airport. I've been here before, or at least next to it on the ground, and I know where it sits. It's not a big runway—seventy-five feet by four thousand feet—but it's the biggest I've landed on today. This should be easy.

"Cessna Two Nine Bravo, Camdenton. Just want to let you know your parents are here."

"Oh, great," I say. "No pressure there. Two Nine Bravo."

"They just want to see how many landings you can get in."

I cross the Osage River branch of the lake and then the Niangua River branch. Lin Creek is off to the left. So many stories here. So many hours on boats. So many hours in the water, on skis, swimming, goofing off, racing.

I descend to pattern altitude. And then I can see it—the runway in front of me. There are PAPI lights to tell me if I'm on the right glide path, and I see four white lights, which means I'm too high, so I point the nose down and go through the routine.

"Camdenton, Cessna Two Nine Bravo on final for one-five, Camdenton."

Carb heat. Flaps. Speed down to 70 knots.

I'm dead-on the glide path, two white lights and two red. Then I see the telephone wires. They have those little red balls attached so there's no way I can miss them. I look at the PAPI lights. I'm exactly where I should be, but I don't like the look of those wires. I've never landed here before, and I don't know how close the glide path will bring me. The sun is setting, and I don't know if one sudden wind could hang me upside down and sparking. So I stay a bit high. Four white lights again.

This is Two Nine Bravo, I think. This is the most wonderful little airplane in the sky. And in the back of my mind I remember a video I saw of a C-130 coming in for what they called a tactical landing. Staying high until the last moment, the plane suddenly pointed its nose toward the ground and dove fast and hard. Leveling off at the last moment, it touched down right on the numbers.

I'm not about to try something like that, I think, but I stay

THE LONG CROSS-COUNTRY

a bit high until I cross the telephone wires and then I push the yoke forward and dive toward the numbers. I level off, flare, and touch down easily. Although I don't see him, my father is standing in the grass between the runway and the terminal, arms raised, two thumbs up. My mother, standing outside the terminal building, is beaming.

The Ride

It takes a moment to get into Two Nine Bravo, but my father can't wait. Once he's in the right seat and the seat belts are connected, I hand him the extra headset. He scans the instruments, though from his side many are difficult to see.

"Ready?" I ask.

"Let's go!" he says.

We taxi back onto the runway, turn to the south, and I push in the throttle. Two Nine Bravo rolls down the centerline, and when we have enough speed I pull back on the yoke. Elegantly we climb over the runway and then back to the right.

We do not have much time. But as soon as we are level and looking at the home ground, I ask if he wants to take the controls. His hands come up immediately.

I know my mother is listening, so I key the microphone. "Camdenton, Two Nine Bravo. Just want to let you know that Fred is flying the airplane."

I can imagine what my mother must think.

We fly over the cut for the new interstate highway. We fly over shopping centers and neighborhoods. We fly over the center of town. We bank gently left and gently right. Forty-five years, give or take, since he last held the controls of an airplane, and every move is as smooth as if he flew yesterday.

Forty-five years, give or take, and he still carries his pilot's license in his wallet.

We turn back toward the airport, and I take over the controls. On final approach I point out the telephone wires, and we do another little dive at the end. The landing is perfect. As we taxi to the spot where I will shut down the airplane, tie her down, and cover the engine with the thermal blanket, I tell my father that he was my very first passenger.

"Really?" he asks.

Really.

My mom comes out to the plane, and we get everything put away and secure. There are a thousand stories to tell from just this last little tour, and a thousand more to tell from the flight to get here. Even though we leave the airport and Two Nine Bravo is quiet, we are three thousand feet over the middle of the country and, at least until we fall asleep, we will never land.

A Note on Sources

One of the real joys of being a writer is the journey so often to some library or someplace on the Internet where stories have already been told. Although it's almost a cliché now to imagine a writer happily surrounded by dusty volumes of old narratives, like all clichés there's also a bit of truth to the image. Very often during the course of writing this book I turned to the histories and the numbers for both illumination and context.

What follows is not a bibliography. In those cases where I simply quoted from some source—most often in the chapter titled "Dreams of Flying"—the authors and book titles suffice. Where the source is a bit more obscure, however, I cite it here.

What Remains
Historical facts are taken from the wonderful *Timetables of History*, by Bernard Grun (New York: Touchstone Books, 1982); *Bonfires to Beacons: Federal Civil Aviation Policy*

under the Air Commerce Act, 1926–1938, by Nick A. Komons (Washington DC: U.S. Department of Transportation, 1978); *Pilot's Directions: The Transcontinental Airway and Its History,* edited by William M. Leary, preface by Wayne Franklin (Washington DC: Government Printing Office, 1921; reprint, Iowa City: University of Iowa Press, 1990); *Western Area Update 6,* no. 3 (March 2007), a newsletter by the U.S. Postal Service; *Safer Skyways: Federal Control of Aviation, 1926–1966,* by Donald R. Whitnah (Ames: Iowa State University Press, 1966); *Aviation's Golden Age: Portraits from the 1920s and 1930s,* edited by William M. Leary (Iowa City: University of Iowa Press, 1989); the North Dakota State Historical Society Web site, http://www.nd.gov/hist/chrono.htm#1932; *Airlines of the United States since 1914,* by R. E. G. Davies (Washington DC: Smithsonian Institution Press, 1972); many phone conversations with Bob Johnson, Bruce Kitt, and Dave Olson at the Northwest Airlines History Office; and a telephone interview with Joe Kimm (August 24, 2007).

The Pilot's Journal
Meriwether Lewis and William Clark, *The Definitive Journals of Lewis and Clark,* edited by Gary E. Moulton, 13 vols. (Lincoln: University of Nebraska Press, 1983–2001).

Bad Form
National Transportation Safety Board aviation accident reports are all quoted from http://www.ntsb.gov/ntsb/Month .asp and the Department of Transportation's Bureau of Transportation Statistics Web site, http://www.bts.gov/.

The Spin

On the Web site for the Aircraft Owners and Pilots Association, there is a page dedicated to the stall and spin: http://www.aopa.org/asf/publications/topics/stall_spin.html.

The World Record

Historical and speed-record information comes from the official Web sites of the Smithsonian Air and Space Museum, the Pikes Peak International Hill Climb, Le Mans, the National Aeronautics Association, the Fédération Aéronautique Internationale, the Indianapolis 500, National Geographic News, National Public Radio, NASA, and Wikipedia.